REVISE EDEXCEL GCSE (9–1)
Business
REVISION GUIDE

Series Consultant: Harry Smith

Author: Andrew Redfern

Notes from the publisher

While the publishers have made every attempt to ensure that advice on the qualification and its assessment is accurate, the official specification and associated assessment guidance materials are the only authoritative source of information and should always be referred to for definitive guidance.

Pearson examiners have not contributed to any sections in this resource relevant to examination papers for which they have responsibility.

For the full range of Pearson revision titles across KS2, KS3, GCSE, Functional Skills, AS/A Level and BTEC visit: www.pearsonschools.co.uk/revise

Contents

Edexcel publishes Sample Assessment Material and the Specification on its website. This is the official content and this book should be used in conjunction with it. The questions in Now try this have been written to help you practise every topic in the book. Remember: the real exam questions may not look like this.

Terms in blue can be found in a glossary on page 93.

The dynamic nature of business

Businesses operate in dynamic markets. New opportunities arise and new businesses and business ideas are created. Wherever there is a need for a product or service, an entrepreneur may take the chance to meet that need with a new business venture.

Changing technology

As new technology develops, new business opportunities arise. New technology can often improve products and services, and make them more desirable in a number of ways. New technology can:

- make products and services **faster**
- make products **smaller** (more compact)
- make products and services **cheaper**
- make products and services **easier to use**
- make products **safer**.

Changing consumer needs

Society is constantly changing. These changes lead to consumers spending their money in different ways. New business opportunities can arise because of new consumer wants and needs caused by:

- changes in **fashions**
- changes in the **economy**
- changes in **national** demographics
- changes in **lifestyle**, such as the way consumers spend their leisure time
- changes in **technology**.

Obsolescence

The introduction of new technology and the changing nature of consumer needs means that products and services can become obsolete very quickly. Many products are designed to only last a short time, and consumers are encouraged to buy newer and improved versions of these products. This is called **planned obsolescence**.

Digital music downloads are an example of how new technology makes products and services obsolete. Physical CD sales in the USA dropped by more than 75% between 2005 and 2014.

Worked example

Give **two** examples of the way in which new business ideas can be generated. **(2 marks)**

1 A new idea, such as a new invention.

2 Developed from existing ideas, such as by making slight changes and improvements to an existing product or service (innovation).

A new business venture can be **unique** (the only one of its kind) or similar to other existing ideas.

Level of uniqueness:
Left highly unique
Right generic business

Unoccupied gap in the market

Entrepreneur thinks they can do it better

Market big enough for another competitor

Now try this

1 Explain **one** opportunity that the introduction of new technology creates for a business. **(3 marks)**

2 Explain **one** way in which a gap in the market creates a business opportunity. **(3 marks)**

Risk and reward

Before an entrepreneur starts their own business or sets up their own company, they will consider the **risks** and **rewards** associated with their business venture. Some businesses may be considered higher risk than others, but they may also offer greater rewards to their owners.

Working out the risk

Risk is worked out by considering the **probability** of a negative outcome occurring and the **impact** of the negative outcome. Starting any business will involve taking a risk because there are so many **unknown factors** that affect long-term business success.

Rewards

Business success – personal satisfaction, excellent products/services, growth, and awards and recognition

Profit – where revenue exceeds costs over a period of time

Independence – many business owners will value the freedom of working for themselves over working for someone else

Starting a business

Risks

Business failure – through poor cash flow, fall in sales revenue or the action of competitors

Financial loss – an owner may lose the capital they invest in the business if it fails. This could include their personal belongings if the business has unlimited liability

Lack of security – not working for someone else means no guaranteed income, sick pay or holidays

> There are both rewards and risks associated with starting a business.

How can risk be reduced?

- Carry out detailed **market research** (you can revise market research on page 8).
- Produce a **business plan** (you can revise business plans on pages 31–32).
- Ensure that the business is **competitive** (you can revise competition on pages 13–14).
- Raise sufficient **start-up** finance (you can revise finance on pages 23–24).

What makes some businesses riskier than others?

- Seasonal demand, such as for ice cream.
- A small market.
- A highly competitive market with lots of competitors.
- An owner who knows little about the product or market.

Worked example

Sonia Fletcher set up as a sole trader selling cakes made from organic ingredients. Which **one** of the following is an example of a risk for Sonia's business?

Select **one** answer:

- ☐ **A** Sonia has estimated that demand will rise over the next six months
- ☒ **B** Sonia has calculated a negative cash flow for August
- ☐ **C** Sonia is anticipating that the cost of flour will fall next year
- ☐ **D** Sonia has estimated that she will need to work an extra 5 hours per week to meet demand for her products

(1 mark)

> Consider the factors that could lead to business failure. Although Option D might be a personal downside for Sonia, it is not likely to cause business failure. Option B is the correct answer as it is a risk for the business.

Now try this

Explain **one** reason why someone might want to set up their own business.

(3 marks)

The role of business enterprise

A **business** or enterprise is a person or organisation with the **purpose** of producing goods and services to meet the needs of customers. A business might produce its own goods or buy them from a supplier and sell them to **customers**.

What businesses do

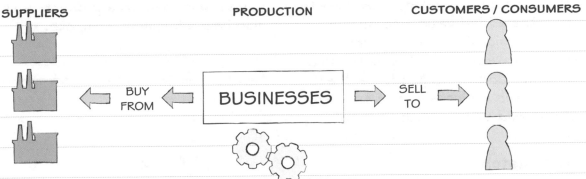

SUPPLIERS   PRODUCTION   CUSTOMERS / CONSUMERS

BUY FROM ← BUSINESSES → SELL TO

Supplier: a business that sells (supplies) products to another business.

Production: using raw materials, labour and machinery to make products.

Customer: a person or organisation that buys the product or service.
Consumer: the person that uses (consumes) the product.

The purpose of all products and services is to meet the needs of customers, often in order to make a profit.

Adding value

Successful businesses will be able to **add value** to their products and services. A business can add value to its product by lowering variable costs or adding something that will make customers willing to pay a higher price.

Adding value is very closely linked to profit.

Ways to add value
- More convenience
- Unique selling point
- Better design
- Improved quality
- Branding
- Greater speed of service

£100	£30 Value added: what the business adds
Price	£70 Variable cost

Worked example

Which **two** of the following might be the best ways in which an oven-cleaning business could add value to its products?
Select **two** answers: **(2 marks)**

- ☐ **A** Employing an accountant to manage cash flow
- ☒ **B** Offering free after-care visits to check customer satisfaction
- ☐ **C** Making sure they have an excellent relationship with the bank
- ☐ **D** Buying a van with the name of the company clearly written on the side
- ☒ **E** Providing a weekend service so that customers do not need time off work

B and E are things that customers would be willing to pay more for. Option B would provide a better all-round service, and Option E would improve convenience. The other three options might improve the business but would not **add value**.

Now try this

Discuss why a business may find it difficult to add value to its products or services. **(6 marks)**

3

The importance of added value

Adding value is important to a business for a number of reasons. A business must decide how best to combine the features of its products to add value.

The benefits of adding value

The added value of a product goes towards paying off a company's fixed costs. The higher the added value, the sooner costs can be paid off and the quicker a business will make a profit. The more value a business can add to its products, the more chance the business has of success, survival and long-term growth.

Unique selling point

A unique selling point (USP) is another way to add value to a product. A USP will also help a business compete.

Developing a USP can be aided through understanding customer needs and market mapping.

Mix and match

Most products combine a range of features to add value and improve competitiveness. The most successful products are the ones that are able to keep costs down as they add new features or benefits.

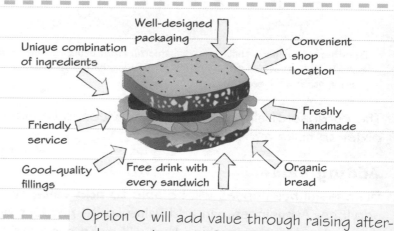

Well-designed packaging

Convenient shop location

Unique combination of ingredients

Freshly handmade

Friendly service

Good-quality fillings

Free drink with every sandwich

Organic bread

Option C will add value through raising after-sales service, and Option D will add value through a stronger brand image. Customers are willing to pay more for these things.

Worked example

Which **two** of the following are strategies that a professional gardener might use to help their business achieve high levels of added value? Select **two** answers: **(2 marks)**

☐ A Ensure a profit is made on every job completed

☐ B Give price discounts

☒ C Visit every customer 48 hours after work is completed to take feedback

☒ D Develop a strong brand awareness in the local area

☐ E Compare the prices of competitors every month

Now try this

Which **one** of the following is most likely to be a reason why a business would try to add value to its products? Select **one** answer: **(1 mark)**

☐ A To increase the materials it buys

☐ B To add a USP

☐ C To differentiate its product

☐ D To improve its chances of survival in the long term

The role of entrepreneurship

An **entrepreneur** is a person who owns and runs their own business. Entrepreneurs are **risk-takers** who have an **initial idea** and the willingness and confidence to see it through.

What do entrepreneurs do?

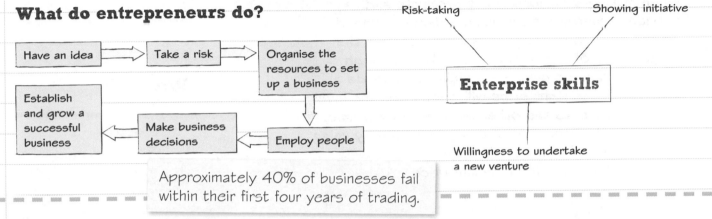

Have an idea → Take a risk → Organise the resources to set up a business → Employ people → Make business decisions → Establish and grow a successful business

Risk-taking   Showing initiative

Enterprise skills

Willingness to undertake a new venture

Approximately 40% of businesses fail within their first four years of trading.

Entrepreneurs innovate

Entrepreneurs create new products through invention and innovation.

RESEARCH AND DEVELOPMENT — INVENTION → POTENTIAL PRODUCTS AND PROCESSES — INNOVATION → PRODUCTS READY TO SELL TO CUSTOMERS

Benefits to the economy

Entrepreneurs benefit the economy by:

* creating products and services to meet people's needs
* creating jobs
* generating economic activity through consumer spending
* paying tax to the government
* exporting goods abroad.

Which **two** of the following are key features of enterprise?
Select **two** answers: **(2 marks)**

☐ **A** Employing at least one worker

☐ **B** Having the right qualifications to run a business

☒ **C** Being prepared to take risks

☒ **D** Having a willingness to take on a new venture

☐ **E** Registering as a private limited company

When answering questions about enterprise, remember that it involves the things required to start a new business.

Now try this

Which **two** of the following are key enterprise skills? Select **two** answers: **(2 marks)**

☐ **A** A willingness to take risks

☐ **B** A willingness to employ at least five workers

☐ **C** A willingness to take the initiative

☐ **D** A willingness to follow a course of study in business

☐ **E** The ability to raise finance

Customer needs 1

If a business is to make products and services that are **desirable** and **profitable**, they must be able to **meet customer needs** successfully. A business that can meet customer needs will encourage **repeat purchase** and **attract new customers**.

What customers want

When making decisions about products and services, customers will make a decision based on the balance of the four factors shown in the diagram. All of the factors are **linked through price**, because a business's ability to provide a product at the right price will depend on the level at which it meets the other factors. For example, improving the standard of product quality by using better-quality raw materials may increase costs, which will have an effect on the price.

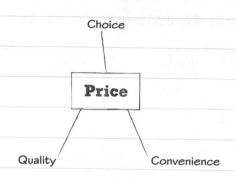

Meeting customer needs

Customer need	Example
Price	Charging a price that is 20% lower than competitors' prices
Choice	A restaurant serving a menu that offers more than 30 different dishes
Convenience	A business offering customers next-day delivery on all items
Quality	A clothes manufacturer using only the highest grade of cotton in all garments

Worked example

Explain **one** reason why a business might sell a wide range of products.　**(3 marks)**

A business would sell a wide range of products to give customers more choice. If customers have more choice, it is more likely that they will find a product that meets their needs. As a result, the business will increase its sales because all customers will find something that they like.

In this answer, the student starts by identifying a reason linked to customer needs. The student then goes on to explain why providing customers with a choice would be beneficial. They have developed the reason with two linked strands of development. You do not need to give context in an 'explain' question.

Now try this

State **one** way that a business could meet customer needs through providing high-quality products.　**(2 marks)**

Customer needs 2

A business cannot treat all of its customers the same way. Customers with similar needs will be influenced in different ways by their **personal circumstances** and **characteristics**. A business must understand the differing needs of its customers so that it can continue to generate sales and survive.

Personal circumstances

Family needs

Customers with children will have different needs from a couple with no children

Financial needs

People with different incomes will choose to buy products and services at different price points

Understanding customers

Personal tastes and preferences

All customers have personal preferences based on style, colour, function and personal taste

Emotional needs

Some customers may have strong emotional connections to certain brands and products

Customer needs and different products

A customer's needs will differ for different types of products. In some cases, the right price may be more important than choice. In other circumstances, it may be the other way around.

For example, a customer buying a short-haul flight to Europe may value price and convenience over quality or customer service. However, the same customer buying a different product, such as a pair of hiking boots, may be willing to pay a high price if they receive excellent customer service (advice from a specialist) and a high-quality pair of boots.

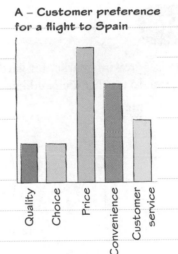

A – Customer preference for a flight to Spain

(bar chart with categories: Quality, Choice, Price, Convenience, Customer service)

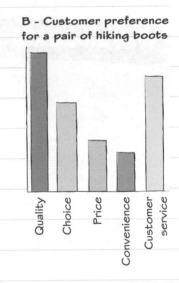

B - Customer preference for a pair of hiking boots

(bar chart with categories: Quality, Choice, Price, Convenience, Customer service)

Worked example

Which **two** of the following are likely to be the most effective methods that an office furniture business might use to meet customer needs?

Select **two** answers: **(2 marks)**

☐ **A** Securing repeat purchases by customers

☒ **B** Fulfilling customer orders quickly

☐ **C** Setting non-financial objectives

☒ **D** Selling furniture at a competitive price

☐ **E** Advertising on local radio

Only Options B and D have anything to do with meeting customer needs.
Option B is an example of convenience and providing good customer service.
Option D is an example of meeting customer needs through appropriate pricing.

Now try this

Which **one** the following is a reason why customer service is important to the success of a small business?

Select **one** answer: **(1 mark)**

☐ **A** Customers are the ones who add value

☐ **B** A small business wants to get repeat purchases

☐ **C** Customers will buy a product if the price is right

☐ **D** It has to meet legal requirements

The role of market research

A business will carry out market research appropriate to its size and the nature of its market. The purpose of market research is to help a business to understand its **customers**, **competitors** and the **market** in which it operates, in order to make informed decisions about its products and services.

Identify gaps in the market or opportunities

Identify and understand customer needs

Identify and understand competitors

The purpose of market research

Understand how well the business is doing, such as customers' opinions of its products

Understand trends in the market, such as market growth

Inform business decisions and reduce the risk associated with making business decisions

Worked example

Lisa Gallagher believes there is a growing market for gardening services. She has conducted some market research to test her idea and has summarised her findings.

Type of household	Percentage
Single – no children	7
Single – with children	11
Single – pensioner	28
Couple – no children	9
Couple – with children	31
Couple – pensioners	14

Table 1

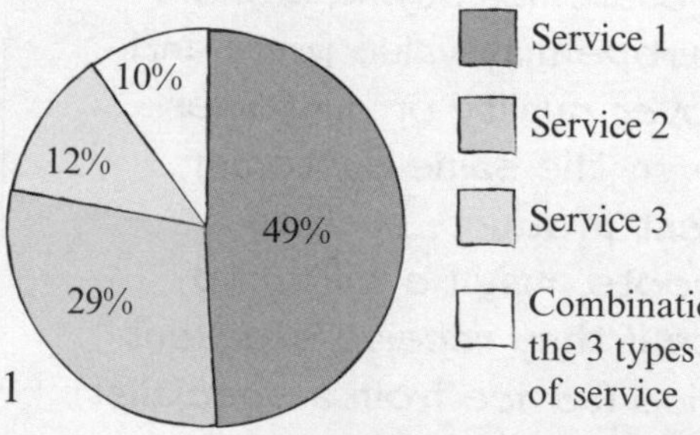

Pie chart (Figure 1): 49%, 29%, 12%, 10%
- Service 1
- Service 2
- Service 3
- Combination of the 3 types of service

Figure 1

Study Table 1 and Figure 1. According to this information, which **two** conclusions can Lisa draw from the data?

Select **two** answers: **(3 marks)**

☒ **A** 100% more single pensioners than pensioner couples are interested in Lisa's business

☐ **B** Lisa should not offer Services 2 or 3 as there is no demand

☐ **C** Her main two segments are couples with no children and singles with children

☒ **D** More than half of people prefer something other than Service 1

☐ **E** Couples with children are more likely to use Service 1

> **Quantitative skills** Make notes on what the data tells you. It is important that you interpret the data correctly before you begin to choose the correct answers. Once you are sure that you understand the data, eliminate the options that you know are incorrect. Why are Options B, C and E incorrect?

Now try this

Discuss why a business may conduct extensive market research before it begins trading. **(6 marks)**

Types of market research

Primary research (field research) is collecting information that did not exist before. This first-hand contact with customers is valuable to a business in understanding its market.

Primary research
- Focus groups
- Observations
- Surveys
- Experiments
- Social media
- Questionnaires

Secondary research (desk research) is the process of gathering secondary data, which is information that already exists.

Secondary research
- Internet sites
- Local newspapers
- Sales data
- Government reports
- Telephone directories
- Market reports

- More accurate
- Up to date
- Specific to needs
- Effective at collecting qualitative data
- Direct customer contact

- More general
- Less time-consuming
- Effective at collecting quantitative data

Many businesses use **social media** as a cheap way to collect information on market trends, customer opinions and the actions of their competitors.

Market research questions

Focus on...	Example questions
Customers	• What do our customers value? • What benefits are offered by our product? • How can we improve our products? • How much are our customers willing to pay?
Competitors	• Who are our closest rivals? • What is their **market share**? • What makes them competitive?
Market	• What is the price of existing products or services? • How many people are buying these products? • Is the market growing or shrinking? • What are the latest trends?

Worked example

Which **two** of the following are the benefits of conducting secondary market research instead of primary market research? **(2 marks)**

Select **two** answers:
- ☐ **A** It adds value to the products
- ☒ **B** It is less time-consuming
- ☒ **C** It offers a wider range of information
- ☐ **D** It is more specific to the target market
- ☐ **E** It will lower the costs of production

Ways of collecting market research data include:
- multiple-choice questions
- yes/no questions
- sliding scales such as 1–10
- customer comments.

Now try this

Which **one** of the following would not be an appropriate method of market research for a new small business? **(1 mark)**

Select **one** answer:
- ☐ **A** Employing a specialist market research company to carry out a survey of 10 000 people
- ☐ **B** Using published statistics about market trends
- ☐ **C** Asking customers to fill in a short questionnaire on the premises
- ☐ **D** Conducting an interview

Market research data

There are two categories of market research data:

- **qualitative** data – information about people's opinions, judgements and attitudes
- **quantitative** data – data that can be expressed as numbers and statistically analysed.

Size and scale

Market research can be **expensive** and small businesses may only do a little. Larger businesses may pay a market research company to carry out extensive primary research. The greater the **sample size** (proportion of the population) used, the more **accurate** the research will be.

Effective market research is likely to link quantitative and qualitative information together. For example, it would help a business understand a 20% fall in customer satisfaction ratings if a focus group revealed that this was due to the layout of the business's new website.

Bias

Bias is the inclination to agree with a particular idea. Market research data can be biased if customers give the answers that they think the business wants them to give, for example when a small business owner collects the opinions of family. Bias also occurs by not surveying a **representative** sample of people. For example, a cafe owner will receive different feedback on his menu from people eating lunch to those just wanting a drink, so only asking those people will result in biased data.

Reliability

In order to make good business decisions, research data should be reliable – it should come from a representative sample of people and the questions should enable people to give accurate and relevant

This leads the customer to agree with the statement so the data would be biased.

People with 0 or 3+ pets cannot answer, so the data would be inaccurate.

✗	✓
Don't you agree that this product should only be available in black? Yes/No	Tick your colour preference for this product. ☐ red ☐ green ☐ black
How many pets do you have? ☐ 1 ☐ 2 ☐ 3	How many pets do you have? ☐ 0 ☐ 1–2 ☐ 3+

Worked example

Apple produces home electronics, including the iPad and iPhone, for the mass market. Product design is an important part of its success.

(a) Give **one** method of collecting qualitative market research. **(1 mark)**

Focus groups

(b) Analyse the impact on Apple of using qualitative market research to improve its understanding of customer needs. **(9 marks)**

Qualitative research will give Apple information about whether consumers think their computers, iPads and iPhones are good-quality products. This will enable Apple to change their product design so that consumers will pay more.

Other methods include interviews, consumer panels or questionnaires/surveys.

This is a good start to a 9-mark 'analyse' question. The student should now develop their answer. This may include at least two different reasons applied to the context of Apple.

Now try this

1 Define the term 'market research'. **(1 mark)**
2 Give **one** way in which a business might collect quantitative market research data. **(1 mark)**
3 Explain **one** way in which market research data might benefit a business. **(3 marks)**

Market segmentation

A **market segment** is a group of buyers with similar characteristics and buying habits. Segmenting a market allows a business to understand its customer needs and to target its customers better.

How to segment a market

A market can be segmented in many ways, based on the characteristics and needs of customers.

In order to accurately segment its market, a business must have a good understanding of its customer needs through effective market research.

Age – e.g. 18–25

Gender – e.g. female

Income – e.g. socio-economic group

Location – e.g. Newcastle

Demographics – e.g. young couple

Lifestyle – e.g. adventurous

Benefits of segmentation

Market segmentation allows a business to:

👍 meet specific customer needs

👍 **differentiate** its products

👍 focus on a specific group of customers

👍 target its marketing activity

👍 develop a unique brand image

👍 build close customer relationships.

Limitations of segmentation

👎 Targeting a range of different customers with different products and services can be costly.

👎 Focusing on one group of customers can cause a business to miss another opportunity.

👎 Customer characteristics change over time, such as lifestyle, income and demographics.

Businesses have to continually update their understanding of their customers as customer needs change over time.

Worked example

Explain **one** way in which effective marketing can help improve the products of a business. **(3 marks)**

If a business understands its customers' needs, its products and services can be developed to meet these needs. This means that the products will be more attractive and desirable, leading to a greater number of sales.

Make sure that you:
- identify **one** way (for example, product development)
- make two further expansion points about the way that you have identified.

Now try this

1 Define the term 'market segment'. **(1 mark)**

2 Explain **one** reason why a business may choose to segment its market. **(3 marks)**

Market mapping

Market mapping helps businesses to position their products by identifying gaps in the market.

Market maps

A market map is a diagram that can be used to position and compare products in a market. It is also used to identify **gaps in the market**, which are opportunities where customer needs are not being met. A market map will compare businesses based on two **variables**, such as price and quality.

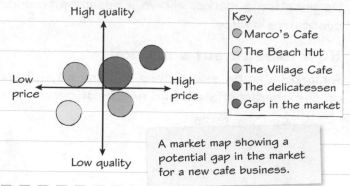

Key
- Marco's Cafe
- The Beach Hut
- The Village Cafe
- The delicatessen
- Gap in the market

A market map showing a potential gap in the market for a new cafe business.

Benefits of market mapping

👍 Helps to identify potential gaps in a market (opportunities).

👍 Helps businesses to identify their closest rivals.

👍 Supports market segmentation.

👍 Helps businesses to make decisions about marketing and positioning its brand.

Limitations of market maps

👎 Based on opinions and perceptions, rather than on accurate data.

👎 Compares businesses based on only two variables, which is simplistic.

👎 Can be difficult to identify the most appropriate variables.

Head-to-head competition

There doesn't always have to be a gap in the market for a business to be successful. Businesses can target the same customers as other businesses and still succeed:

☑ if there is enough demand in the market (enough customers)

☑ if the business is able to meet customer needs better than its competitors (by offering more choice or better customer service).

Worked example

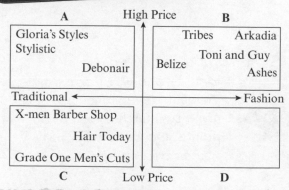

According to the market map, which **one** of the following describes a gap in the market? **(1 mark)**

Select **one** answer:

☐ **A** High price / traditional

☐ **B** High price / fashion

☐ **C** Low price / traditional

☒ **D** Low price / fashion

Option D is the only quadrant where there are no other businesses.

Now try this

Which **two** of the following are **most likely** to be important in spotting a new business opportunity in the cycling market? Select **two** answers: **(2 marks)**

☐ **A** Being able to produce a product cheaply

☐ **B** Recognising a new gap in the market

☐ **C** Being a keen cyclist

☐ **D** Identifying the possible competitors

☐ **E** Having a large amount of personal savings

Competition

A business might use a number of criteria to analyse the **strengths** and **weaknesses** of its **competition** in order to adjust its business offering and **differentiate** its products and services.

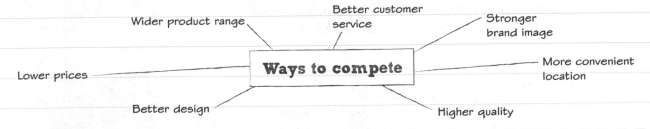

Wider product range

Better customer service

Stronger brand image

Ways to compete

Lower prices

More convenient location

Better design

Higher quality

Differentiation

Product differentiation is about making a product different from others in some way. It helps businesses:

- to position their products and target different market segments
- to gain an advantage over rivals when faced with competition.

It allows consumers to see clearly that their needs are being met more effectively by one product than by another.

How to differentiate products

Instead of competing head-to-head, businesses can try to differentiate their products.

Head-to-head competition

BUSINESS → PRICE > PRICE ← COMPETITOR

Differentiation

QUALITY

BUSINESS   COMPETITOR

CUSTOMER SERVICE

Worked example

Which **two** of the following methods are mostly likely to differentiate a driving school from its rivals?

Select **two** answers: **(2 marks)**

☒ **A** Providing high-quality tuition

☐ **B** Operating as a sole trader

☒ **C** Providing a personalised service

☐ **D** Operating in a competitive market

☐ **E** Providing a service for the community

Options A and C are ways in which a business can differentiate what it does.

Now try this

Which **two** are the most likely methods that a small independent music store might use to compete with a large supermarket chain that also sells CDs?

Select **two** answers: **(2 marks)**

☐ **A** Lower its prices below that of the supermarket

☐ **B** Launch an advertising campaign on national television

☐ **C** Provide an ordering service for hard-to-find CDs for their customers

☐ **D** Open up two new stores in the town

☐ **E** Focus on improving the quality of customer service

Competitive markets

What is a competitive market?

A market is **competitive** when there are a large number of businesses relative to the number of potential customers. Competition is also high in markets where businesses sell very similar products and services that are difficult to differentiate.

The market for sugar is highly competitive because there is little difference between one producer's sugar and another's. This means that businesses mainly compete on price, although quality may also be considered. On the other hand, cakes and confectionary products can be highly differentiated, allowing businesses to compete in different ways.

Competition and business decision-making

Some of the decisions that a business might make in a highly competitive market include:

- improving efficiency
- finding ways to improve competitiveness
  (see page 13 to revise competition)
- differentiating its products and services
- lowering its prices
- giving customers special offers
- cutting costs.

Drawbacks of highly competitive markets

A business that operates in a highly competitive market might have to:

- lower prices in order to compete
- accept lower profit margins
- cut back on expenditure
- be careful about how and when it expands
- monitor its competitors closely.

Consumers benefit from competition as it encourages businesses to lower their prices and also to improve quality and customer service.

Worked example

Explain **one** reason why a business might decide to lower the price of its products. **(3 marks)**

A business might decide to lower its prices in order to remain competitive against other businesses. If a business lowers its prices, it will seem more appealing to customers compared to other alternatives. As a result, customers may choose it over rivals and its sales revenue may increase.

The student has explained how price is one way that a business might compete against rival businesses. An 'explain' question does **not** require you to analyse the benefits and drawbacks (e.g. the fact that the business might also lower its profit margins by reducing its prices).

Now try this

1 State **one** possible method a business could use to differentiate its product. **(1 mark)**

2 Explain **one** reason why a differentiated product might benefit a business. **(3 marks)**

Aims and objectives

All businesses set **objectives**. Sometimes these are financial objectives, which can be expressed in money terms. Businesses also have non-financial objectives. These are more personal and may involve helping others.

The objectives hierarchy

Aims are the general goals that a business sets. An aim can be the purpose for a business's existence.

Objectives are more specific than aims, but they contribute to a business achieving its aims. Objectives can be either financial or non-financial.

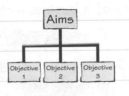

Most businesses will have an overarching aim that is supported by a number of SMART objectives, often specific to functions of the business.

Typical objectives for a start-up

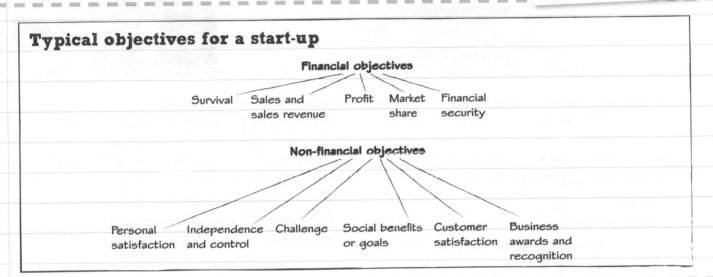

Financial objectives

Survival Sales and sales revenue Profit Market share Financial security

Non-financial objectives

Personal satisfaction Independence and control Challenge Social benefits or goals Customer satisfaction Business awards and recognition

---

Worked example

Which **two** of the following are the most likely reasons why an individual would want to start a business?

Select **two** answers: **(2 marks)**

☒ **A** To use the profits of a business to make a difference

☐ **B** To work fewer hours each week

☐ **C** To avoid paying income tax

☐ **D** To show their boss that they are as good as them

☒ **E** To control their own future

Both Option A and Option E are examples of non-financial objectives. Option A involves helping others, while Option E is about independence and control (being your own boss). Options B–D are not really viable objectives for starting a business.

Now try this

Which **one** of the following is the most likely reason why Sonia decided to set up a business?

Select **one** answer: **(1 mark)**

☐ **A** She wanted to have more spare time

☐ **B** She wanted to have more independence when making business decisions

☐ **C** She wanted to make a guaranteed profit

☐ **D** She wanted to reduce the number of risks she had to take

Differing aims and objectives

As a business develops and grows, so do the ambitions of the entrepreneur or owner who runs it. This means that different businesses have different aims and objectives. It also means that the aims and objectives of a business change, depending on its current stage of development.

Business A

Business B

Business A has been running for six months. It has started to gather a loyal **customer base** and to receive **repeat purchases**. Initial customer reviews are positive.

Business A's objectives are to:

- survive
- have independence and control
- achieve 100% customer satisfaction
- achieve financial security.

Business B is a chain of 15 stores nationwide. It has been established for 12 years and in the last five years has become the second largest of its type in the market. It is a **public limited company** (PLC). Turn to page 50 for more on PLCs

Business B's objectives are to:

- become market leader
- achieve a sales revenue of £200 million
- donate 1% of all profits to charity.

These objectives are appropriate for Business A because many small businesses fail within the first few years of opening. The owner wants the independence of running their own business. Customer satisfaction is very important if the business is to grow.

These objectives are appropriate for Business B because a large successful business may have a realistic ambition to become market leader. Its success over the last 12 years and its **shareholders** will mean that the business will have profit targets. As a large business, it may also wish to give something back to society by donating to charity.

Worked example

Explain **one** reason why a business would set financial objectives.   **(3 marks)**

A business would set a financial objective because most businesses are judged on their financial success. If the objective is to increase revenue as a percentage of sales (units) then this would be a quantifiable objective and easy to measure. Increasing revenue increases the likelihood of the business making a profit.

The student has explained why financial performance is important to a business and how a financial objective linked to revenue would to help achieve this.

Now try this

1 Give **one** example of a non-financial objective.   **(1 mark)**

2 Define the term 'market share'.   **(1 mark)**

Revenues and costs

A business must understand the difference between the price it charges to customers and the cost of producing its products. If it knows how many products it sells, it can calculate its total revenue and its total costs. It can then calculate profit.

 **Calculating revenue**

Revenue, sales revenue or **turnover** is the amount of income received from selling goods or services over a period of time. It can be calculated using the formula:

 Revenue = Price × Quantity

Fixed and variable costs

✓ **Fixed costs** do not vary with the output produced by a business, e.g. business rates.

✓ **Variable costs** change directly with the number of products made, e.g. raw materials.

 Variable costs = Cost of one unit × Quantity produced

 **Total costs**

Total costs are all the costs of a business. It can be calculated using the formula:

Fixed costs, e.g. business rates

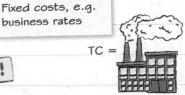

TC =

Total costs (TC) = Total fixed costs (TFC) + Total variable costs (TVC)
£900 = £400 + £500 = £400 + (£5 × 100)

Variable costs, e.g. wages

Worked example

Hancock's is a small pottery business that specialises in garden plant pots. It has the following financial information for one month.

Number of pots produced and sold: 150

Average price per pot: £10   Fixed costs per month: £500

Variable costs per pot: £2

Which **one** of the following represents the total costs for Hancock's during the month?

Select **one** answer: **(1 mark)**

☐ **A** £450   ☒ **C** £800

☐ **B** £650   ☐ **D** £1500

 Be careful. You could arrive at an incorrect answer to this question if you use the numbers incorrectly in your calculation.

Now try this

The following table shows the costs, revenues and profits of a cleaning company for a two-month period. Complete the table with the **four** missing figures.

(4 marks)

	October	November
Revenue	£14 000	£12 000
Fixed costs	£2000	£2000
Variable costs	(i)	(iii)
Total costs	£9000	(iv)
Profit	(ii)	£5000

Profit and loss

A business must be able to calculate whether it is making a profit or loss. It must also understand how making a profit or loss can have an impact on the business and its owners.

📊 Quantitative skills — Profit and loss

Profit occurs when revenues of a business are greater than its total costs. If a business's costs are greater than its revenues then it will make a loss. Profit or loss can be calculated using the formula:

LEARN IT!   Profit = Sales revenue − Cost of sales

Profit or loss = 💰💰 − 🏭 👷

£1000 − £900 = £100 profit

> There are two different kinds of profit: gross profit and net profit. You can revise these on page 73.

Profit as an objective

Profit is the objective of many businesses because it allows a business to:

- survive
- reinvest profits for expansion
- provide security and savings
- reward employees
- generate wealth for the owner.

Profit can also act as an incentive to start the business.

📊 Quantitative skills — Calculating interest on loans

In your exam, you may be required to calculate the total interest to be paid on a loan.

LEARN IT!

$$\text{Interest (on loans) \%} = \frac{\text{Total repayment} - \text{Borrowed amount}}{\text{Borrowed amount}} \times 100$$

Interest rates

Interest is the % reward for saving

Saving £

Borrowing £

Interest is the % cost of borrowing

Worked example

Which **two** of the following actions is most likely to increase a pottery business's profit, assuming that it sells the same number of pots each month? Select **two** answers: **(3 marks)**

☒ **A** Buy cheaper raw materials to make its products

☐ **B** Increase the number of workers employed over the weekend

☐ **C** Buy more expensive raw materials to make its pots

☐ **D** Increase advertising expenditure

☒ **E** Relocate to cheaper premises

📊 Quantitative skills

Options B, C and D would actually increase the business's costs. Options A and E would lower costs.

Now try this

A business spent:
- £10 000 on raw materials
- £30 000 on fixed costs
- £7500 on other variable costs and had a turnover of £50 000.

The business now buys its raw materials 10% more cheaply from a new supplier. What effect will this have on profit?

Select **one** answer: **(1 mark)**

The profit level will:

☐ **A** Increase by £2500

☐ **B** Fall by £2500

☐ **C** Increase from £2500 to £3500

☐ **D** Increase by 10%

Break-even charts

Break-even is the level of output at which a business's revenue covers its total costs. At this point the business is making neither a loss nor a profit. Break-even is an important financial concept as it allows a business to make important decisions about prices, sales volumes and costs.

The point on the graph where total costs and revenue meet is the **break-even point** or **break-even level of output**. When **total revenue** exceeds the break-even point, the business makes a **profit**. When total revenue falls below the break-even point, the business makes a **loss**.

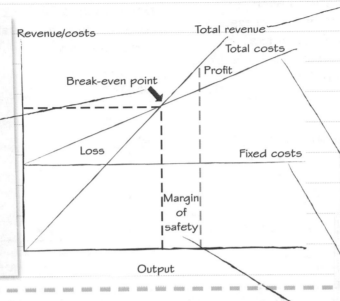

Total revenue is the amount of money earned by a business from selling products. It increases directly with the number of products sold.

Total costs are the sum of all the costs at any level of output.

The **fixed costs** line is horizontal because fixed costs do not change at any level of output.

Quantitative skills   **Formulae to know** **LEARN IT!**

Revenue = Price × Quantity

Total costs (TC) = TFC (total fixed costs) + TVC (total variable costs)

Break-even point in units = $\dfrac{\text{Fixed cost}}{(\text{Sales price} - \text{Variable cost})}$

Break-even point in revenue / costs = Break-even point in units × Sales price

The **margin of safety** is the amount of output between the actual level of output where profit is being made and the break-even level of output. This is how much production could fall before the business starts to make a loss.

Worked example

Using the information below, calculate Sony's break-even point when its PlayStation 4 console was priced at £300. You are advised to show your workings.

Fixed costs: £2 400 000

Variable costs: £140 per console   **(2 marks)**

Break-even = Total fixed costs ÷ (Price − Variable cost per item).

Break-even = £2 400 000 ÷ (£300 − £140)

Break-even = 15 000 consoles

Quantitative skills

Make sure you:
- show accurate workings
- calculate the correct answer.

Now try this

Using the information below, calculate the level of profit or loss Sony would make if it sold 20 000 PlayStation 4 consoles at £300 each. You are advised to show your workings.

Fixed costs: £2 400 000   Variable costs: £140 per console   **(2 marks)**

Using break-even

Break-even analysis is a useful tool to help a business make decisions, set targets and plan for the future.

Break-even analysis is a useful tool for answering 'What if?' questions such as: what would be the impact of an increase in variable costs on profit? A fall in fixed or variable costs or an increase in price is likely to lower the break-even point.

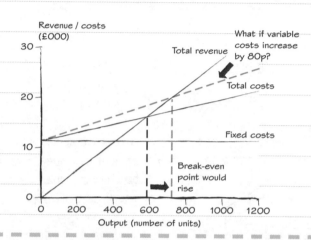

Lowering the break-even point

Break-even analysis can identify strategies for lowering the break-even point and increasing profit.

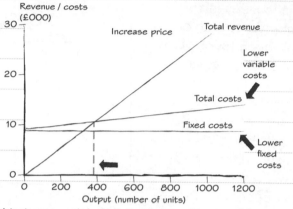

A business can only lower the break-even point successfully so long as productivity, quality and demand are not compromised. For example, although increasing price will lower the break-even point, some customers may be put off and choose a product from a competitor.

📊 Quantitative skills — Interpreting break-even charts

The break-even point: where the total revenue and total costs lines intersect, read the number of units required to break even from the x-axis (e.g. 1000 units).

The margin of safety: subtract the break-even point (in units) from the actual or predicted level of output/sales (e.g. 700 units).

LEARN IT!

$$\text{Margin of safety} = \text{Actual or budgeted sales} - \text{Break-even sales}$$

Caution! The concept of break-even assumes that a business will sell all the products it makes. In reality, if a business increases price it will lower the break-even point, but might deter customers from buying.

Worked example

Discuss the reasons why a business might use a break-even chart. **(6 marks)**

When launching a new product, a business could use a break-even chart to identify the number of units it must sell in order to cover its costs. Using this information, a business can then make decisions on how many units it will need to produce and carry out market research in order to understand whether it believes there is sufficient demand to sell this number as a minimum...

Now try this

A business is using a break-even chart to examine the effect of a reduction in the price of its product.

1 State **one** problem a business may face as a result of reducing the price. **(1 mark)**

2 Explain **one** limitation for a business of using a break-even chart. **(3 marks)**

This student has identified a reason and developed their explanation. They could now go on to develop a second reason with further development.

Calculating cash flow

Cash flow is the money flowing into and out of a business on a day-to-day basis. A **cash-flow forecast** predicts how cash will flow through a business over time. A business can use it to identify periods where it could have a **cash flow problem**.

Cash-flow forecasts

Inflows / receipts – e.g. money from owners, bank loans or cash from sales.

Outflows / payments – e.g. wages, raw materials, interest on loans, advertising or bills.

Net cash flow (negative or positive) – the receipts of a business minus its payments. Net cash-flow = cash inflows - cash outflows in a given period (learn it)

	SEPT	OCT	NOV	DEC
Total receipts	8000	8500	13500	15000
Payments				
Machinery and equipment	10000	0	0	0
Wages and materials	4400	4400	6000	4000
Heating, lighting, and insurance	0	3500	1000	0
Total payments	14400	7900	7000	4000
Net cash flow	−6400	600	6500	11000
Opening balance	0	−6400	−5800	700
Closing balance	−6400	5800	700	11700

Opening balance – the amount of money in a business at the start of a month (the previous month's closing balance).

Closing balance – the amount of money in a business at the end of a month (net cash flow + opening balance).

Worked example

Complete the table with the **four** missing figures.
(4 marks)

	Jan	Feb	Mar
Receipts (£)	10000	8500	15000
Payments (£)			
Raw materials	2000	2500	3600
Fixed costs	4000	4000	4000
Other costs	5000	5200	5900
Total payments	**11000**	**11700**	**13500**
Net cash flow	−1000	−3200	1500
Opening balance	500	−500	−3700
Closing balance	−500	−3700	−2200

Quantitative skills An exam question could ask you to fill in the blanks on a cash-flow forecast. Use the following to help you.
- **Receipts** – Add net cash flow and total payments.
- **Payments** – A missing payment could be found by adding up the rest and taking it away from total payments.
- **Total payents** – Add up all payments or subtract net cash flow from receipts.
- **Net cash flow** – Subtract total payments from receipts or deduct the closing balance from the opening balance.
- **Opening balance** – This is always the previous month's closing balance.
- **Closing balance** – Add the net cash flow to the opening balance.

LEARN IT! Cash flow is calculated as (Receipts – Payments = Net cash flow) + Opening balance = Closing balance

Now try this

A business has the following cash-flow information for one particular month.
Opening balance: £5000 Cash inflow: £7000 Cash outflow: £14000
Which **one** of the following is the closing balance for the business at the end of the month?
Select **one** answer:
(1 mark)

☐ **A** −£12000 ☐ **B** −£2000 ☐ **C** £9000 ☐ **D** £16000

The importance of cash to a business

It is important for a business to understand the factors that affect its cash flow and also how cash flow problems can lead to insolvency.

The importance of cash

Without sufficient cash within the business, a business would become **insolvent**. This means that it would be unable to:

- pay its suppliers and other debts
- repay bank loans
- pay wages to employees
- buy raw materials and products to sell
- promote the business.

Cash versus profit

Cash is not profit. Cash is the given amount of money that is available for a business to use to pay its debts. Profit is an absolute calculation involving total revenue and total costs over a period of time. A profitable business can still fail if it experiences cash flow problems. This is because revenue is recorded before the business receives actual cash. Similarly, cash does not have to be spent on costs at the point at which the costs are recorded.

Change in sales revenue / change in demand

Change in costs (e.g. commodity prices)

Credit terms can change (e.g. period of time or amount needed to pay a bill or invoice)

What impacts on cash flow?

Seasonality in sales (e.g. sun cream)

Change in stock levels

Business expansion or contraction

Worked example

Which **two** of the following are the most likely ways that PrintZone Ltd could improve its cash flow position? Select **two** answers: **(2 marks)**

☐ **A** Use a mind map to improve financial planning
☐ **B** Carry out quantitative market research
☒ **C** Increase revenue by improving sales
☒ **D** Negotiate lower prices with suppliers
☐ **E** Employ two more full-time members of staff

Which options would either increase cash inflows or slow down cash outflows?

Interpreting cash-flow forecasts

(£)	April	May	June
Receipts	3400	4500	5000
Payments	4000	4200	4200
Net cash flow	−600	300	800
Opening balance	−300	−900	−600
Closing balance	−900	−600	200

A cash-flow forecast

A negative net cash flow means that cash outflows are greater than cash inflows for that month. This means the business will have cash-flow problems if it does not have enough cash in the bank (its opening balance) to cover its payments. A business must make financial arrangements to resolve cash-flow problems if it forecasts a negative closing balance.

Now try this

Discuss how a business could improve its cash flow.
(6 marks)

Short-term sources of finance

Small businesses need **finance** for a range of reasons. It might be needed to pay for starting up the business in the first place or to expand the business. Sources of finance can be categorised into **short term** and **long term**. A business's choice of source will be based on its requirements.

Reasons for finance

There are many reasons why a business might need a new source of finance, such as:

- paying for expenses (e.g. wages)
- expanding the business
- investing in new products and services
- starting a new business
- paying for any unforeseen costs.

Short-term versus long-term finance

Short-term sources of finance are repaid immediately or quite quickly (usually within a year) and are used for costs such as buying stock or paying a utility bill.

Long-term sources of finance are usually repaid over a longer time period (even up to 25 years). Long-term sources would be used to finance a new business or to expand a business.

A business that is expanding usually requires new sources of finance.

Short-term sources of finance

Source	Good for...
Bank overdraft	covering short-term expenses that can be repaid quickly.
Trade credit	paying for stock or goods later (e.g. after 30 or 60 days), when the goods have already been sold.

Finance and cash-flow problems

You should know the causes of cash-flow problems and have some ideas about how a business could improve its cash flow. Short-term sources such as trade credit and overdrafts are suitable solutions to help solve cash-flow problems.

Worked example

Which **one** of the following would be the most appropriate action for a business in order to cope with its negative cash-flow forecast for August and September?

Select **one** answer: **(1 mark)**

- ☐ **A** Approach its bank to take out a loan
- ☐ **B** Sell more shares in the company
- ☒ **C** Arrange an overdraft with its bank
- ☐ **D** Seek out the services of a venture capitalist

Negative cash flow is an immediate issue, so it requires a short-term source of finance to resolve the problem. The overdraft in Option C is the only short-term source of finance mentioned.

Now try this

Explain **one** reason why a business might use a bank overdraft. **(3 marks)**

Long-term sources of finance

Different long-term sources of finance

	Good for...
Personal savings	covering short-term expenses that can be repaid quickly.
Venture capital	raising capital from investors to fund a new business idea.
Share capital	raising large amounts of money by selling **equity** in a limited company.
Loan	covering large expenses associated with starting or expanding a business, which will be repaid over a number of years.
Retained profit	reinvesting in a successful business to ensure that it keeps growing.
Crowd funding	raising money from a large number of people in return for some sort of reward (e.g. products, involvement or ownership).

Selling shares

A share is a part-ownership in a business. A limited company can sell **shares** to potential investors to raise capital. These investors are then **shareholders** in the business and are entitled to a share of any profits generated.

Share capital (800 shares)

Shareholder X
400 shares allotted (50% ownership)

Shareholder Y
400 shares allotted (50% ownership)

Crowd funding

Crowd funding is the process of raising small amounts of money from a large number of customers for a new project, product or **start-up**.

Worked example

Which **two** of the following are long-term sources of finance for a sole trader?

Select **two** answers: **(2 marks)**

- ☒ **A** Profit
- ☐ **B** Overdraft
- ☒ **C** Bank loan
- ☐ **D** Trade credit
- ☐ **E** Share capital

Options B and D are **short-term sources** of finance (you can revise short-term sources of finance on page 23). This leaves Options A and C as correct long-term sources. Option E is not an option for sole traders.

Now try this

Which **two** of the following would be the **most appropriate** sources of finance for a hairdresser intending to set up as a sole trader?

Select **two** answers: **(2 marks)**

- ☐ **A** Personal savings
- ☐ **B** Selling the business's assets
- ☐ **C** Issuing shares to new shareholders
- ☐ **D** Retained profit
- ☐ **E** Bank loan

Limited liability

The term 'liability' refers to the legal responsibility of a business towards its debts.

Unlimited liability

Owner and business are the same

Sole traders (or sole proprietors) are businesses owned by one person. The owner has **unlimited liability**. The owner is legally responsible for any debts of the business. Therefore there is potential for the owner to lose his or her personal belongings to pay off any debts.

Limited liability

 Business is a separate entity from owner (it may only exist on paper)

Private limited companies (Ltd) have **limited liability**. The owners and the business are separate legal entities. Any debts incurred by the business belong to the business and the owners can only lose money up to the amount that they have invested. Their personal belongings are not liable.

Differences between limited and unlimited liability ownership

	Unlimited liability	Limited liability
Risk	Unlimited liability means there is more risk.	Limited liability reduces the risk for the owners.
Control	The owner has 100% control of decisions.	The amount of control held by the main owner depends on the proportion of the business sold as shares to other shareholders.
Profits	The owner keeps 100% of the profits.	Profits are shared between shareholders in proportion to the number of shares that they hold.
Privacy	Accounts do not have to be made public.	Accounts are filed with Companies House and can be viewed by anyone on payment of a small fee.

Worked example

Which **two** of the following might be the most likely reasons why someone might set up as a private limited company?
Select **two** answers: **(2 marks)**

- ☐ **A** She wants to raise lots of money on the stock exchange
- ☒ **B** She believes the risk would be less than operating as a sole trader
- ☐ **C** She wants to be the sole owner of the business
- ☐ **D** She would have access to limited sources of finance
- ☒ **E** She would be liable only for the amount she invested if the business failed

Option A is incorrect, as a private limited company is not allowed to sell its shares through the stock market. Options C and D do not apply to a private limited company.

Now try this

Which **one** of the following is a disadvantage of unlimited liability for a sole trader?
Select **one** answer: **(1 mark)**

- ☐ **A** Needing to pay higher taxes
- ☐ **B** Less control of the business
- ☐ **C** Sharing profit with other shareholders
- ☐ **D** Risk of losing personal possessions

Types of business ownership

When starting a business, an entrepreneur has a number of options for their business's legal status. Their choice may depend on a number of factors, including finance, size, security and privacy.

Categories of ownership

You can revise public limited companies (PLCs) on page 50.

```
                        Business ownership
                       /                  \
              Limited liability      Unlimited liability
              /            \           /          \
  Private limited    Public limited  Sole traders  Partnerships
  company (Ltd)      company (PLC)
```

Advantages and disadvantages of different types of business

Type of ownership	Advantages	Disadvantages
Sole trader	👍 Sole trader makes all of the decisions. 👍 Quick and easy to set up. 👍 Sole trader keeps all of the profits. 👍 Financial information is kept private.	👎 Unlimited liability. 👎 Harder to raise money to start or grow the business. 👎 A lot of pressure on one person. 👎 No one to cover when sole trader is ill or takes time off.
Partnership	👍 Owners may have wider expertise and can share ideas and decision-making. 👍 Owners share the risk. 👍 Could be easier to raise finance to establish or grow the business.	👎 Decisions made by one partner can affect all partners. 👎 No longer exists if one partner leaves. 👎 Profits are shared. 👎 Partners may disagree.
Private limited company	👍 Owners have limited liability. 👍 Customers may trust a 'Ltd' more than other businesses. 👍 Continues to trade even if the shareholders change. 👍 Could be easier to raise finance to establish or grow the business.	👎 More complex to set up than a sole trader or partnership. 👎 Shareholders may disagree. 👎 Financial information is published and can be accessed by others. 👎 More information must be reported to the government.

Worked example

Explain **one** reason why a business owner may want to set up a partnership. **(3 marks)**

One reason why a business owner might want to set up a business as a partnership is because they can share the responsibility of running the business with someone else. This will reduce the risk of running the business and make it easier for the business to succeed in the long term.

This student understands the benefits of running a partnership and has developed two advantages to having a shared responsibility in the business.

Now try this

1 State **one** drawback of running a private limited company. **(1 mark)**

2 Define the term 'limited liability'. **(1 mark)**

Franchising

A **franchise** is the right given by one business to other businesses to sell goods or services using its name. The businesses that buy into a franchise remain independent businesses.

Who's who?

✅ **Franchisor** – the business that gives franchisees the right to sell its product or service.

✅ **Franchisee** – a business that agrees to manufacture, distribute or provide a branded product under licence from a franchisor.

The principle of franchising

Franchising is the expansion of an established business by licensing the right for **entrepreneurs** to set up their own business using the name, equipment and products of the franchise. In return, the franchisee pays the franchisor a fee or share of the sales revenue.

What does the franchisee get when they buy a franchise?

A franchise is like buying a ready-made business in a box.

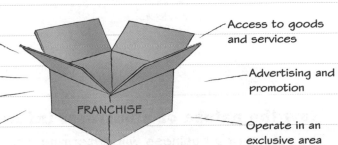

An established brand name

Training

Equipment

Ongoing support

FRANCHISE

Access to goods and services

Advertising and promotion

Operate in an exclusive area

Benefits of running a franchise

👍 Brand image and reputation is already established.

👍 Expensive marketing costs are covered by the franchise.

👍 Access to tried-and-tested products.

👍 May have an established customer base.

👍 Higher chance of survival.

👍 Specific support and training provided.

Drawbacks of running a franchise

👎 The cost of the initial investment can be high.

👎 The owner has little freedom to make decisions.

👎 Franchisee will have to pay a fee or **royalty** (percentage of sales revenue) to the franchisor.

👎 Restrictions on where the franchise can be set up.

Worked example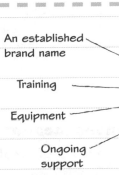

Which **one** of the following is a type of organisation set up 'under licence' to use an established business name?

Select **one** answer: **(1 mark)**

☐ **A** Sole trader   ☒ **C** Franchise

☐ **B** Enterprise   ☐ **D** Private limited company

Now try this

Explain **one** drawback of running a franchise.   **(3 marks)**

Business location

Location is a key decision when setting up a business. Location is more important for some businesses than for others. The significance of different factors in the choice of location also varies between businesses.

Proximity

The location's proximity or nearness to various factors is a key consideration for most businesses.

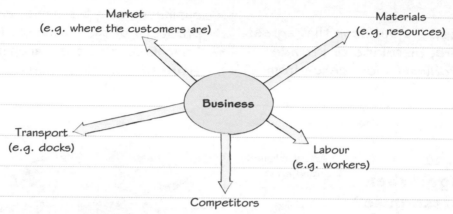

Market
(e.g. where the customers are)

Materials
(e.g. resources)

Business

Transport
(e.g. docks)

Labour
(e.g. workers)

Competitors

How the nature of a business influences location

The nature of a business will determine which factors of location are the most important.

Nature of business	Influences
Manufacturing	May require specialist resources to be transported to their site and specialist facilities for removal of waste, e.g. away from local residents.
Exporting	May need access to docks, rail or airports in order to distribute goods abroad.
Retailing	May need to be situated on a busy high street to gain the benefits from passing trade and being located in an area where customers tend to shop.
Tourism	May need to be near popular tourist attractions such as beaches and famous landmarks.

Location and the internet

Trading on the internet (e-commerce) removes the significance of location for many businesses because the place where they trade is virtual. For some businesses, this allows them to save costs, because the business's premises do not need to be in busy city centres or close to the market that they serve.

All five factors are relevant to location, but Options B and C are the most important for a manufacturer of complex goods that is likely to employ a lot of workers.

Worked example

Which **two** of the following are the most important factors of location for a car manufacturer? **(2 marks)**

Select **two** answers:

☐ **A** Proximity to car insurance businesses
☒ **B** Proximity to suppliers
☒ **C** Proximity to labour market
☐ **D** Proximity to a city centre
☐ **E** Proximity to competitors

Now try this

Discuss why some businesses may choose a business location on the outskirts of a large city. **(6 marks)**

The marketing mix

Marketing involves identifying and understanding customers' needs and wants. Businesses then use the **marketing mix** (4 Ps) in order to provide products and services that meet these needs while generating a profit for the business.

The 4 Ps

 Product

The **product** itself has to meet the needs of customers and have the correct attributes and features that the customer wants. A successful business will differentiate their products from their competitors' products.

You can revise the importance of product on pages 59–60.

 Place

Place is the way in which a product is distributed (how it gets from the producer to the consumer). Businesses have to consider the channel (e.g. online or through retail stores). For example, a luxury suit might be sold in an upmarket boutique on Bond Street in London.

See page 65 for more on the importance of place.

 Promotion

Promotion is communication between the business and customer that makes the customer aware of the business's products, including:

• advertising
• sales promotions
• sponsorship
• public relations.

You can find out more about the importance of promotion on page 63.

 Price

The **price** of a product must reflect the value customers place on the product. High-quality products have a high price. Customers are also willing to pay more for special features. Price is very subjective because it depends on many factors.

Turn to page 61 to revise the importance of price.

Worked example

Lisa believes there is a market for gardening services and has carried out market research. Some of her research results are shown below.

What is the most important factor in the decision to choose a gardening service?	
	Number of responses as a percentage
Price of the service	12
Quality of the work	41
Advertisement in the local paper	16
Customer service	20

According to the table, which **one** element of the marketing mix should Lisa focus on when marketing her business?
Select **one** answer: **(1 mark)**

☐ A Place
☐ B Price
☒ C Product
☐ D Promotion

The table shows that '**quality of the work**' and '**customer service**' receive the highest responses. These two factors contribute to the 'product' that Lisa's gardening business provides.

Now try this

1 Explain **one** reason why a business would charge a higher price for a product or service. **(3 marks)**
2 Explain **one** reason why a business might choose to use social media to promote its products. **(3 marks)**

Influences on the marketing mix

Balancing the marketing mix

High-quality prestigious timepiece

Premium price

Product ⟷ Price

Promotion ⟷ Place

Lifestyle magazines, TV adverts and prime position billboards

Approved jewellers, with centre position in display windows

A business must develop an integrated marketing mix where each P **complements** the others.

Changing needs

A business may **adapt** its marketing mix so that it continues to meet the changing needs of customers and the competitive environment, by:

- changing the **features** of a product to incorporate new trends and technology
- adjusting the **price** of its products in response to competitors' pricing
- launching a new **advertising** campaign to boost interest in response to falling sales
- selling its products through popular **retailers**
- allowing customers to **return** online products free of charge.

The impact of technology on the marketing mix

New technology demands that products are constantly innovated, especially in tech industries that produce items such as computers and smartphones.

Many businesses are switching their focus from traditional advertising mediums to forms of digital communication such as social media sites.

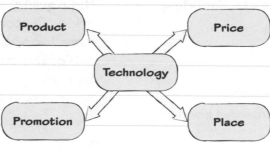

Product → Price

Technology

Promotion → Place

Customers can easily compare prices online – businesses have to monitor rivals to remain competitive.

E-commerce not only provides an effective channel for selling, but also the ability to customise products and services. Businesses must balance 'clicks' with 'bricks'.

Worked example

Explain **one** reason why place is an important aspect of the marketing mix. **(3 marks)**

If a business gets 'place' right, it will make their products more accessible to customers. As a result, it is likely that there will be greater customer awareness, which could lead to increased sales over time.

This answer includes a reason with two logical chains of development to score all three marks. You do **not** need to refer to a particular business or context when answering 'explain' questions.

Now try this

Chocolicious is a small business making handmade chocolates. It operates in a very competitive market but one competitive advantage is the quality of its chocolates. There has been a recent rise in the price of cocoa. In response to this, Chocolicious has decided that it needs to change its marketing mix.

Which **two** changes to the marketing mix would you advise, given what is happening in this market?

Select **two** answers: **(2 marks)**

☐ **A** Reducing its corporation tax payments

☐ **B** Producing a new business plan

☐ **C** Contacting supermarkets to seek new retailers for its products

☐ **D** Making five members of staff redundant to cut costs

☐ **E** Finding a cheaper supplier for its ingredients

The business plan

A **business plan** is a plan for the development of a business, giving forecasts of items such as sales, costs and cash flow.

The purpose of a business plan

A business owner may write a business plan to:

- convince a bank to loan the business money
- forecast financial projections
- identify the needs of customers
- formulate market research into important information, e.g. about competitors
- provide information, e.g. about competitors
- provide the owner with a 'plan of action' that will minimise risk.

The contents of a business plan

The business plan links together topics covered in different parts of the specification. For example, a business plan will include a cash-flow forecast and business objectives. It will also help an entrepreneur to answer important questions about their business, such as 'what if?' questions, which will help to reduce the risk of starting a business.

Who uses a business plan?

Owners – as a guide and working document

Lenders – e.g. banks will want to investigate the likely success and risk of lending to a new business

Partners and employees – anyone wanting to work with/for the business

Investors – to assess the risk and reward of investing in the business (e.g. Ltd or Plc)

Worked example

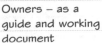

Which **two** of the following would Marie have had to include in her business plan?

Select **two** answers: **(2 marks)**

- ☐ **A** All her invoices and receipts from purchases and sales
- ☐ **B** A copy of the design of her business card
- ☒ **C** A cash-flow forecast
- ☐ **D** A record of all her profits from the business for the past five years
- ☒ **E** An overview of the nature of the business

In this answer, Options A and D are not feasible, as Marie would not have this information before she started her business. Neither are these financial records necessary in a business plan. Option B is irrelevant, as a design of a business card would provide little useful information. Options C and E are both examples of relevant information normally included in a business plan.

Now try this

Which **two** of the following are the most likely reasons to produce a business plan?

Select **two** answers: **(2 marks)**

- ☐ **A** To show off the skills of the entrepreneur
- ☐ **B** To get support from a bank
- ☐ **C** To show other people you can create a business plan
- ☐ **D** To convince customers to buy from the business
- ☐ **E** To help monitor actual sales against forecast sales

The nature of business planning

The contents of a business plan

Any good business plan should at least contain the following information.

Element of business plan	Details
Business idea	An outline of the business idea and concept so that all stakeholders can understand the owners' intentions.
Aims and objectives	Aims and objectives that are **SMART** (specific, measureable, achievable, realistic and time-bound). This means that the business can measure its success against these targets.
Market research	Market research that identifies the business's target market as well as market conditions and any other competitors.
Financial forecasts	Forecasts of the business's costs, revenue, profit, cash flow, budgets and break-even point.
Sources of finance	How the business will be financed and how any borrowings will be repaid.
Location	The location of the business and the reasons for that choice of location.
Marketing mix	How the business will use the marketing mix to develop a successful product or service.
Production	How the product will be produced, including suppliers.

Risk and planning

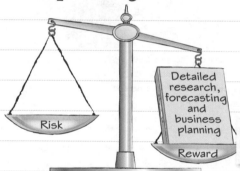

An entrepreneur can never be 100% certain that they are making the right decisions when starting a business. However, detailed business planning reduces the risk associated with unforeseen problems and poor decision-making, and increases the likelihood of success.

Good forecasting and planning reduces the level of risk and swings the balance in favour of reward.

Worked example

Discuss the reason why a business would include market research in a business plan. **(6 marks)**

One reason why a business owner would include market research in a business plan is that market research will show potential lenders that the owner understands the market they are selling to and this might reduce the risk of lending the business money. For example, understanding customer preferences and what they are willing to pay means the business is more likely to produce a product or service that customers desire....

This is just part of a student answer.

The student has started by explaining one reason why market research is an important element of a business plan. This answer has then been developed. The student has also given an example to illustrate their point. This is a good approach to take when answering a 'discuss' question. The student could now go on to discuss how market research will help the business owner understand the competition in the market in order to make relevant decisions when planning.

Now try this

Explain **one** reason why a business would include financial forecasts in a business plan. **(3 marks)**

Stakeholders

A **stakeholder** is an individual or a group that has an interest in and is affected by the activities of a business.

Owners (shareholders) – want profits and a return on their investment

Managers – want bonuses and long-term success

Pressure groups – want to influence business decisions and actions

Stakeholders

Employees – want good pay and working conditions

Suppliers – want regular orders

Government – wants low unemployment and competitive markets

Local community – wants local investment and limited pollution

Customers – want value for money

A business has an impact upon and can be affected by its stakeholders. This means that business decisions must take into account stakeholder needs.

The impact of stakeholders

Local community complains about traffic congestion

Bad publicity leads to falling sales

In order to maintain profits for owners, employee bonuses are withheld

Employees are unhappy with fall in incomes

Business guarantees employees' bonuses in the following year by raising prices

Customers are unhappy with prices and sales fall further

As a result, the business halves its usual order value from suppliers

All stakeholders are linked. The actions of one stakeholder group are likely to have an impact on other groups, and it is difficult for a business to meet everyone's needs.

Worked example

The Elm Tree is a successful traditional pub in the village of Elmton and is owned by Jeremy Cousins. He has decided to use land behind the pub to build a private function room for weddings and events.

Which **one** of the following stakeholders is the extension most likely to have a negative impact on? Select **one** answer: **(1 mark)**

☐ **A** Customers   ☐ **B** Government   ☒ **C** Local residents   ☐ **D** Employees

Each stakeholder is relevant to Jeremy's business. The correct answer is Option C because the local residents may be concerned that building work in their village could cause noise and disruption.

Now try this

Cantwell's is a business that makes zips for clothing. It decides to make five workers redundant.

Which **one** of the following stakeholders is most likely to benefit from this decision? Select **one** answer: **(1 mark)**

☐ **A** Suppliers and the business because they will now sell more zips to Cantwell's

☐ **B** The local community because there will now be more spending in local shops

☐ **C** The government because it will now collect more in tax

☐ **D** The owners because their costs will fall

Stakeholder conflict

Different stakeholders often have different **perspectives** and **interests** in a business. Their interests can be in conflict and some stakeholders can have more influence on decision-making than others.

Business stakeholders

Different stakeholders will have different interests in the performance of a business.

Stakeholder	Key interests
Shareholders	Profit, dividends and growth
Workers	Wages, job security and good conditions
Customers	Fair price, choice and good quality
Managers/directors	Pay, growth and power
Government	Competition and tax revenues
Local community	Jobs and clean environment
Pressure groups	Socially responsible and ethical business behaviour

Stakeholder conflict

Conflicts are likely to occur between stakeholders if they have different interests.

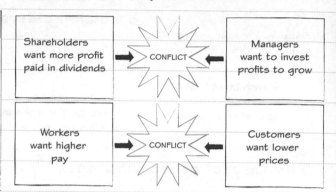

Possible positive effects on stakeholders

👍 Shareholders receive a return on their investment.

👍 Employees and managers receive income, rewards, financial security and status.

👍 Customers receive high-quality products at reasonable prices with excellent service.

👍 The local community may benefit from development and investment in the local area.

👍 The government collects income tax and corporation tax.

Possible negative effects on stakeholders

👎 The local community can suffer because of pollution in the local environment.

👎 The government needs to monitor and regulate business activity that is unfair, anti-competitive or illegal.

👎 Employees may lose their jobs and income or face job uncertainty.

👎 Employees work under poor conditions.

👎 Shareholders lose their investment.

👎 Pressure groups protest against unethical business activity and damage the business's reputation.

Worked example

Change4Life is a government project that encourages people to adopt a healthier lifestyle. Part of the project allows those aged under 18 and over 60 to swim for free in public swimming pools.

State **two** stakeholders that might benefit from the Change4Life project. **(2 marks)**

1 Customers   2 Employees

Now try this

Gerrard PLC announced that it would abandon its plans to build a new chemical-processing plant near West Walton, Teesside. This followed a protest by local residents claiming that the effect on the local environment would be 'catastrophic'.

1 'Define the term 'stakeholders'. **(1 mark)**

2 Explain which group of stakeholders has the most influence on decision-making in this case. **(3 marks)**

Technology and business

Technology drives change in many businesses and creates new opportunities for growth. Businesses use technology to gain a **competitive advantage** over their rivals and often invest in new technology in order to keep up with developments in their specific industries.

E-commerce

Social media

Types of technology that influence business activity

Electronic payment systems

Digital communication (e.g. email and QR codes)

> Make sure you know some specific examples of technology and how it has influenced a business.

Technology and change

New technologies are constantly developing. This creates new opportunities, new markets and new industries for businesses. Investment in new technology can be a huge cost for many businesses, but failing to keep up with the latest technology can lead to loss of competitiveness and business failure. However, the development and adoption of new technology can lead to a competitive advantage for some businesses.

How technology influences business activity

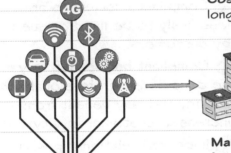

Costs – technology can be a huge investment for businesses, but in the long term it can help a business improve efficiency and reduce costs.

Sales – innovating products with the latest technology can increase demand from customers and boost sales. The means by which a business sells its products can also evolve through e-commerce and digital communication.

Marketing mix – technology influences all aspects of the marketing mix: from lowering the costs of products, to making promotions easier through social media, to allowing customers to purchase products anytime and anywhere through e-commerce.

New technology

Worked example

Explain **one** reason why a business may choose to invest in the latest technology.

(3 marks)

One reason why a business may choose to invest in the latest technology is to increase its competitiveness. By having the latest technology, the business may be able to make its products cheaper, meaning that it can pass these savings on to the customer through lower prices. This will lead to higher sales if prices are lower than their competitors'.

> This is a good answer. The student has given a reason and developed their answer well by using logical chains of development that explain the consequences of investing in new technology.

Now try this

Discuss the likely benefit to a business of using digital communications to communicate with its customers.

(6 marks)

Principles of consumer law

Consumer law governs all aspects of how a business interacts with its customers. The purpose of this legislation is to protect consumers. It is worth learning some examples of relevant legislation for use in the exam, but you do not need to know the specific details of any piece of legislation.

Consumers have the right to return or reject goods.

Goods should be delivered and installed safely.

Products sold to consumers should be of a good standard and quality.

Principles of consumer law

Terms of contracts should be fair.

Businesses should disclose full information about products and services.

Services should be provided with reasonable care.

The consumer protection law in the UK is the Consumer Rights Act 2015.

Impact of consumer law

Drawbacks

👎 Businesses must know the law and keep up to date.

👎 Laws can restrict businesses from operating as they would wish.

👎 Changing products and practices to comply with laws can be costly.

👎 Bad publicity can result if businesses do not comply with laws.

👎 Consumers can use law to take legal action against the business.

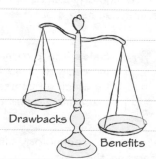

Drawbacks

Benefits

Benefits

👍 Compliant businesses are less likely to be fined or sued by customers.

👍 Compliant businesses may be considered professional and caring, and may benefit from increased customer loyalty.

👍 Improved relationship with stakeholders.

👍 Good publicity, if followed.

Worked example

Evaluate whether Pepsi is right to use the words 'raw' and 'natural' in relation to its new product. **(12 marks)**

...Ultimately it depends on how honest Pepsi is about its advertising of new products and whether customers feel that it is acting ethically. This type of language is used all the time by drinks manufacturers and most consumers will understand that a soft drink is never going to be as healthy as water. Therefore, Pepsi is not really doing anything wrong by using these phrases because the consumers are not being misled and no consumer protection laws are being breached.

Make sure you:
• use the information provided in the exam to support your argument
• use your understanding of consumer protection law
• make a judgement with clear justification.

The last part of this answer has made good use of the 'it depends' rule to show balance in the conclusion.

This is just part of a student answer.

Now try this

Explain **one** disadvantage to a business of the government introducing new consumer protection legislation.

(3 marks)

Principles of employment law

Employment law governs all aspects of how a business interacts with its employees. The purpose of this legislation is to protect employees. It is worth learning some examples of relevant legislation for use in the exam, but you do not need to know the specific details of any piece of legislation.

Recruitment procedures should be fair and prevent discrimination.

All employees' pay should be fair and meet minimum wage requirements.

Groups of people, such as employees with disabilities, should not be discriminated against.

Principles of employment law

Health and safety requirements in the workplace should be met.

Disciplinary issues and grievances should be dealt with fairly.

Redundancy procedures should be fair.

Examples of employment law include the Health and Safety at Work Act 1974, Equality Act 2010, National Minimum Wage (Amendment) Regulations 2017 and Employment Relations Act 1999.

Impact of employment law

Drawbacks

👎 Meeting health and safety regulations can be costly for businesses.

👎 Paying the national living wage will increase businesses' costs.

👎 Failing to comply may lead to unhappy employees, low productivity and legal action.

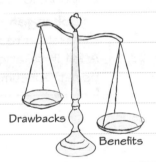

Drawbacks

Benefits

Benefits

👍 A compliant business may be considered a good employer.

👍 Fewer employees will be tempted to leave the business, so reducing recruitment costs.

👍 Employees may be happier and more motivated, leading to high productivity and better customer service.

How businesses meet the requirements of consumer and employment law

 Costs – meeting legal requirements means that businesses incur additional costs.

 Pay – all pay must meet the national requirements for the living wage.

 Equipment – health and safety equipment is required to keep employees safe.

 Administration – businesses must use correct processes and record-keeping systems, e.g. recording health and safety incidents and testing products.

 Licences – businesses must meet legal requirements to be granted relevant licences, e.g. electrical installation licences for electricians.

 Training – employees must be trained in health and safety rules and customer service guidelines.

Now try this

Explain **one** disadvantage to a business of the government introducing new employment protection legislation.

(3 marks)

The economy and business

The economic climate is the level of demand and spending within the economy. Many variables contribute to consumer spending and demand, e.g. the level of economic activity and interest rates. Economic activity is measured by **gross domestic product (GDP)**.

The level of demand in the economy

The **level of demand** refers to spending that takes place in an economy. Demand can come from **consumers, government, business** or **overseas**.

You need to know how the level of demand can affect businesses.

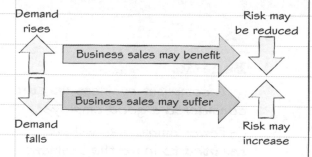

Demand rises → Business sales may benefit → Risk may be reduced

Demand falls → Business sales may suffer → Risk may increase

What might change demand?

Demand in the economy may go up or down because of:

☑ **The level of economic activity** – if there is a recession, demand will fall

☑ **Interest rates** – if interest rates fall, borrowing and demand will increase

☑ **changes in exchange rates** – if the pound gets weaker, foreign demand will rise

☑ **consumer income** – when the economy is doing well, people earn more money and have more disposable income

☑ **changes in taxation** – an increase in most forms of taxation reduces consumers' disposable income. A fall in taxation will have the opposite effect and boost consumer demand for most goods.

Impact of high demand/ economic activity

- Consumer incomes rise
- Inflation may rise
- Unemployment may fall
- Interest rates may rise
- The pound may become stronger

You can revise:
- inflation on page 39
- unemployment on page 39
- interest rates on page 40
- exchange rates on page 41.

Impact of low demand/ economic activity

- Consumer incomes fall
- Inflation may fall
- Unemployment may rise
- Interest rates may fall
- The pound may become weaker

Worked example

Which **one** of the following is likely to reduce consumer spending?
Select **one** answer:

☐ A A fall in interest rates
☒ B A fall in employment
☐ C A fall in the rate of inflation
☐ D A fall in the value of the pound

Option B is the only answer that is likely to have the direct impact of lowering consumer spending. This is because fewer people will have jobs. Note that Option B refers to a fall in **employment**, not **unemployment**.

Now try this

Explain **one** reason why a fall in consumer confidence might affect demand.

(3 marks)

Unemployment and inflation

Unemployment is a problem for the economy and can have an impact on businesses. Inflation can also have a significant impact on businesses.

What is unemployment?

Unemployment exists when people who want to find work cannot do so.

Unemployment can be measured by counting the number of people who claim unemployment benefits or the number of people in a survey who say they are looking for work.

Impact of unemployment on businesses

1 High levels of unemployment may make it easier for businesses to recruit new employees. However, over time, the number of employees with the skills that businesses need will fall.

2 High levels of unemployment lower consumer demand for most businesses' products and services.

3 Economic activity falls when unemployment is high. This means that businesses' sales revenue will also fall.

What is inflation?

Inflation is the change in the average level of prices in the economy. It is measured using the consumer price index (CPI). It measures changes in the price of food, housing, clothing and other products.

Impact of inflation on businesses

☑ A sharp rise in the rate of inflation will cause a business's costs to rise unexpectedly. This can have a direct impact on profits.

☑ Consumers' costs rise when the rate of inflation rises. This reduces consumers' disposable income, meaning that they buy fewer goods and services from businesses. When an increase in inflation causes a business's costs to rise, the business has two choices. It can either absorb the costs or pass them on to its customers by raising prices.

Worked example

Explain **one** effect of inflation on a business.   **(3 marks)**

A rise in raw material prices can cause a firm's costs to rise. Rising costs of production will reduce the firm's profits. This may result in the firm increasing its prices to remain profitable.

There must be a clear explanation of how a rise in inflation can affect a business, using links between points. In this answer, the student has explained how costs, profits and prices are affected.

Now try this

Explain **one** way in which a business might be affected by high levels of unemployment.   **(3 marks)**

Interest rates

An **Interest rate** is the percentage reward or payment over a period of time that is given to savers on savings or paid by borrowers on loans.

The cost of borrowing

An entrepreneur or small business may not have capital to start or expand a business without borrowing. Typically a bank will give a **loan** to a business or allow it to have an **overdraft**. The business will pay **interest**:

- on top of its repayments for the loan
- on any amount it is overdrawn.

This is the cost of borrowing money and the incentive for a bank to lend it.

Fixed and variable interest rates

Fixed interest rates do not change over the life of a loan. A business could lose out on a fixed contract if the rate falls.

Variable interest rates change over the life of a loan. They can be more risky and are hard for a business to plan against.

Rising interest rates

A **rise** in interest rates will **increase** the cost of borrowing.

☑ Businesses on a variable rate may struggle to repay loans.

☑ Small businesses are less likely to borrow money to start up or to expand.

☑ Customers are less likely to spend money as borrowed money costs more, so consumer spending falls.

Falling interest rates

A **fall** in interest rates will **lower** the cost of borrowing.

☑ Businesses will have more money to spend and cash flow may improve.

☑ Businesses may borrow money for a start-up or expansion.

☑ Customers are more likely to borrow and to spend their money. Consumer spending rises.

Worked example

During Sonia's first year of trading, interest rates increased from 3% to 5%. Identify **two** possible effects of this on her business.

Select **two** answers:
(2 marks)

☐ **A** A reduction in fixed costs due to lower repayments on her overdraft

☐ **B** A rise in sales due to higher levels of consumer spending

☐ **C** A greater chance of rivals entering the market

☒ **D** A fall in sales due to lower levels of consumer spending

☒ **E** An increase in fixed costs due to higher repayments on her overdraft

An increase in interest rates is generally a bad thing for small businesses.

Now try this

Explain **one** effect on a small business of an increase in interest rates.

(3 marks)

Exchange rates

The **exchange rate** is the price of buying foreign currency. It tells UK people and businesses how much foreign currency they get for every pound.

📟 **Quantitative skills** | **Calculating the cost of foreign exchange**

Exports: Goods and services sold abroad.

£1 = $2

£500 of goods sold to a business in the USA cost $1000 (500 × 2)

Imports: Goods and services bought from abroad.

$2 = £1

$600 of goods bought by a UK business cost £300 (600 ÷ 2)

The relationship between the exchange rate and importers/exporters

The effect of a fall in the value of the pound	The effect of a rise in the value of the pound
Good for UK exporters of goods – price of exports falls ➡ sales increase.	Bad for UK exporters of goods – price of exports rises ➡ sales fall.
Good for UK tourism – prices cheaper to foreigners ➡ tourism increases.	Bad for UK tourism – prices more expensive to foreigners ➡ tourism falls.
Good for UK businesses – imports more expensive ➡ people buy more UK goods.	Bad for UK businesses – imports cheaper ➡ people buy fewer UK goods.
Bad for UK importers of materials – imports more expensive ➡ costs rise.	Good for UK importers of materials – imports cheaper ➡ costs fall.

Worked example

A business has the following costs in June.

	June
Raw materials imported from USA	£10 000
Raw materials from UK	£7000
Fixed costs	£11 000
Exchange rate	£1 = $1.50

In June the business makes £11 000 profit. In July, the exchange rate has changed to £1 = $1.60.

Assuming all other data remain the same, which **one** of the following effects does this change have on the business's profit level?

Select **one** answer:

(1 mark)

☐ **A** Decrease by £1350

☐ **B** Remain the same

☒ **C** Increase by £625

☐ **D** Increase by £1600

📟 **Quantitative skills** In June £10 000 of raw materials actually costs $15 000 (10 000 × 1.5). In July the business still requires $15 000 worth of raw materials, but as the pound is now stronger it will cost only £9375 ($15 000 ÷ 1.6). Costs have therefore fallen by £625 (£10 000 – £9375). Assuming everything else remains the same, this will increase profit by £625.

Now try this

If the pound weakens, which **one** of the following is most likely to occur?

Select **one** answer:

(1 mark)

☐ **A** International trade will cease

☐ **B** The price of imports will rise

☐ **C** The price of imports will fall

☐ **D** The price of exports will rise

External influences

Just as a business must adapt in response to **internal influences**, such as the development of new products or recruitment of new employees, it must also adapt to **external influences**. These may include the economic climate, legislation, competition, technology and society.

Opportunity or threat?

A business can see any external influence as either an opportunity or a threat. Opportunities could lead to business growth, whereas businesses may have to respond to threats by adjusting their operations.

External influence

Opportunities
- A rise in economic activity, leading to increased demand
- New legislation that increases demand for a business's safety products
- New technology that lowers the cost of production
- Lower interest rates, making it easier for a business to borrow money

Threats
- New competitors entering the market
- New legislation that makes a business's products illegal
- A fall in economic activity, leading to lower demand
- A new technology that makes a business's products obsolete

Cut investment and spending when economic activity is low

Stop producing a product line that has become obsolete due to rise of new technology

Change company policy to adhere to employment or consumer legislation

Invest heavily in new technology in order to gain an advantage over competitors

Responses to external influences

Lower prices to counteract the entrance of a new competitor

Increase productivity and recruit new employees when economic forecasts look positive

A business can either decide to respond to or to ignore external influences. A business cannot adapt to every change, so it is important to make the right decision when choosing which influences to respond to.

Worked example

Which **two** of the following are likely effects on a small business of a downturn in the business cycle?

Select **two** answers: **(2 marks)**

☐ **A** Higher sales owing to rising consumer incomes

☒ **B** Lower fixed costs owing to lower interest rates

☐ **C** Less risk of the business becoming insolvent

☐ **D** More difficulty recruiting employees

☒ **E** Lower demand owing to business closures

Quantitative skills In a downturn there is likely to be a fall in spending. This may result in closures and falls in prices. The government may act in a downturn by lowering interest rates.

Now try this

Discuss how a business might respond to a fall in economic activity.

(6 marks)

Case study

In Sections B and C of Paper 1, you will have to review a full-page case study before answering questions. You should aim to spend about 10 minutes reading the case study before you attempt to answer any questions. Have a look at the sample case study below, then look at the worked examples on the next five pages.

The Wood Fired Pizza Company

Joe is the owner of The Wood Fired Pizza Company based in Sheffield. The company makes authentic pizza and homemade food cooked on a portable pizza oven that provides catering at outdoor events. The Wood Fired Pizza Company can be hired for a variety of events including festivals, corporate days, parties and weddings.

The Wood Fired Pizza Company uses only the finest ingredients that are either grown locally or imported from Italy. The menu lists about 20 different varieties of pizza and customers have the option to design their own creation for a special event. Joe only requires a small space to set up the oven, food preparation and service area. At full heat, the oven can cook a pizza in two-three minutes, meaning that delicious fresh food can be provided with a fast and simple service. The Wood Fired Pizza Company is fully insured and all employees have the necessary food preparation and hygiene qualifications.

Joe uses social media to promote his business and shares the positive reviews the company receives. **Figure 2** shows a customer review on social media.

Figure 1: Company logo

'We hired this company for our daughter's christening. What can we say other than absolutely fantastic!!! Lovely friendly guys. Extremely tasty pizzas that remind us of Italy. Every single person kept going back for more. We would definitely use this company again in the future and would highly recommend them to friends and family. Many thanks!'

Figure 2: A customer review

Joe has produced the break-even chart shown in **Figure 3**, illustrating the costs and revenues for a typical one-day event. The average price of a pizza sold at an event is £8. The variable cost to produce one pizza is £2.

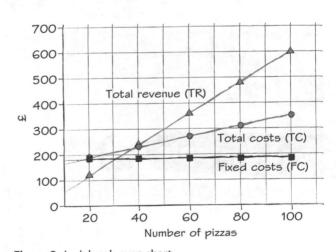

Figure 3: Joe's break-even chart

Now try this

Read the case study above.

(a) Highlight all of the key business terminology in the case study.

(b) Identify **three** factors that might be a unique feature of The Wood Fired Pizza Company.

(c) List the benefits and the drawbacks of Joe's business.

Short-answer questions 1

Worked example

Identify the break-even point for The Wood Fired Pizza Company. **(1 mark)**

30 pizzas

 Draw a dotted line vertically down from the point where TR and TC meet. This is the break-even point.
Make sure you check your answer by using the calculation for break-even:
Fixed costs (FC) / Contribution per unit

$$\frac{180}{6} = 30$$

'Identify' questions

An 'identify' question requires you to interpret information from a source, such as a table or graph (in this case, the break-even chart presented in **Figure 3** on page 43).

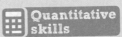 The student has correctly interpreted the break-even point on the graph. Break-even is the point at which total costs are equal to total revenue. Note that break-even is expressed in terms of units (in this case, pizzas).

 Turn to pages 19 and 20 to revise break-even.

'Outline' questions

An answer to an 'outline' question should always give a point with some form of development or explanation. The answer must also be in the context of the provided case study.

The student has identified a relevant way that the company meets customer needs linked to the case study. They have then developed their answer with a point of explanation and an example.

 To revise customer needs, turn to pages 6 and 7.

Worked example

Outline **one** way that The Wood Fired Pizza Company meets customer needs. **(2 marks)**

The Wood Fired Pizza Company meets customer needs by offering customers an extensive range of pizzas on its menu. This helps it meet customer needs because most people will be able to find a type of pizza that they like, for example a vegetarian option.

Worked example

Calculate the profit that The Wood Fired Pizza Company would make if they sold 65 pizzas at a typical event. **(2 marks)**

LEARN IT!

Profit = Total revenue − Total costs
Total revenue = 65 × £8 = £520
Total costs = £160 + (65 × £2) = £290
Therefore profit = 520 − 290 = **£230**

 You can revise profit on page 18.

'Calculate' questions

Always start your answer to a 'calculate' question by writing down the relevant formula so you know what you are doing. Make sure that you learn all of the formulae you need for Paper 1 and Paper 2.

Now try this

Outline **one** reason why it is important for a business like The Wood Fired Pizza Company to provide a flexible service. **(2 marks)**

Your answer should be in the context of The Wood Fired Pizza Company.

Short-answer questions 2

'State' questions

A 'state' question requires you to give a short answer that is no longer than a sentence. Your answer will need to be in context.

The student's answer identifies a relevant method of segmentation appropriate to the context of the business.

 Links Turn to page 11 to revise market segmentation.

 Worked example

State **one** way that The Wood Fired Pizza Company might segment its market.

(1 mark)

The Wood Fired Pizza Company could segment its market based on the type of event it is catering for, e.g. weddings.

 Worked example

Define the term 'social media'. **(1 mark)**

Social media refers to websites and apps that let people and businesses connect with each other to share information and pictures, e.g. Twitter.

The key term that you have to define will be in the case study. If you are unsure of the definition, see how the term is used within the context. This might give you a clue.

'Define' questions

'Define' questions require you to give an accurate definition of a key term. All the key terms you should understand are highlighted in this revision guide. An imperfect definition that is partly right can still achieve both marks if a relevant example is used in support.

The student has given a clear and concise definition of social media with at least two relevant points and an appropriate example.

 Worked example

Calculate the total contribution for 80 pizzas. **(2 marks)**

Total contribution = Total revenue − Total variable costs  **LEARN IT!**

Total revenue = 80 × 8 = 640

Total variable costs = 80 × 2 = 160

Total revenue − Total variable costs = Total contribution

640 − 160 = **£480**

📇 Quantitative skills Always show your workings clearly. Even if you give an incorrect answer, you may be awarded 1 mark for a partially correct calculation.

Links Look at the glossary on page 93 for definitions of key business terminology.

Reading the question

Note that the question requires you to calculate total contribution, **not** the contribution per unit (1 pizza). Students often mix up contribution per unit and total contribution. Contribution per unit is used to calculate break-even.

📇 Quantitative skills The student has used the information to first calculate the total revenue if 80 pizzas were sold. They have then calculated the total variable costs and subtracted this from the total revenue.

 Now try this

The Wood Fired Pizza Company would like to improve its cash flow.
State **one** way in which The Wood Fired Pizza Company could improve its cash flow.

(1 mark)

'Analyse' questions

Worked example

Analyse the impact of The Wood Fired Pizza Company having limited liability.   **(6 marks)**

Improving an answer

Limited liability refers to the legal status of a business. A company has limited liability because the owner's liability is limited to the money that they invested in the company. The impact of The Wood Fired Pizza Company having limited liability is that Joe cannot lose his personal belongings such as his house or car if the business fails. This means that Joe is protected and can be more confident about expanding the business, knowing that his personal belongings are safe. Furthermore, a limited company looks more professional and trustworthy. This may help Joe attract customers to hire his business for events.

Having limited liability does not guarantee that a business will be successful. Customers may have more trust in a limited company but it is still subject to the pressures that all businesses face. The fast food events market is very competitive and there are likely to be many different businesses that provide a similar service to The Wood Fired Pizza Company because it is relatively easy to set up a business of this format with low fixed costs.

> **'Analyse' questions**
> An 'analyse' question is very similar to the 'discuss' question that you will answer in Section A of Paper 1 and Paper 2. However, the key difference is that an 'analyse' question requires you to answer in the context of the case study provided.

This is **not** a model answer. It is a sample answer for you to improve.

The opening sentence defines the term 'limited liability'. This is a good approach to an 'analyse' question as it demonstrates straight away that the student understands the concept mentioned in the question.

This part of the answer explains the benefit of limited liability. However, although it mentions Joe, this paragraph contains little context. There are no significant issues drawn from the case study.

The second paragraph analyses the limitations of limited liability. The student has explained that limited liability will not necessarily protect the business from failure. The second paragraph is also placed in context by referring to the competitive nature of the fast food market and the type of business. The student has also referred to the low level of fixed costs, which has been interpreted from the break-even chart. A good answer will always be rooted in the issues raised in the case study.

Links To revise limited liability, turn to page 25.

Now try this

How else could you improve this student's answer by linking it to the context of The Wood Fired Pizza Company? Try to identify two issues that you might connect when answering this 'analyse' question.

'Justify' questions

'Justify' questions

A 'justify' question requires you to consider two different options. This might include considering the relative benefits and drawbacks of two alternative strategies. Your answer will need to be in the context of the case study and must finish with a justified conclusion based on your analysis.

The question mentions making the business 'competitive'. Always highlight the key terms in the question and ensure that you address them in your answer.

This is **not** a model answer. It is a sample answer for you to improve.

Always try to use business terminology in your answers, e.g. 'premium price' and 'contribution per pizza'.

The student has identified a benefit ('cheaper') and explains why ('not have to be transported so far').

The student goes on to discuss the benefits of Option 2 in the next paragraph.

This paragraph gives the student's conclusion. In it, they have made a decision and provided a justification for their decision. They have also compared the relative merits of Options 1 and 2.

 Links You can revise the concept of tariffs on page 55.

Balance

Balance means identifying the benefits and drawbacks in your answer. Using balance is a good technique to include when answering 'justify' and 'evaluate' questions.

Worked example

The Wood Fired Pizza Company can purchase its ingredients via two options.
Option 1: Grown locally
Option 2: Imported from Italy
Justify which one of these two options would most help The Wood Fired Pizza Company to be more competitive.   **(9 marks)**

Improving an answer

The benefits of Option 1 is that purchasing locally grown produce will help support local businesses. Many people who buy their pizzas might feel strongly about supporting local businesses, therefore this could attract potential customers. Furthermore, some people may be willing to pay a premium price for a Wood Fired Pizza Company pizza knowing that they will be supporting the local economy. Another benefit of local produce is that it is likely to be far cheaper than produce grown in Italy because it does not have to be transported so far. This could reduce unit costs and increase the contribution per pizza...

...Overall, I believe it is better for The Wood Fired Pizza Company to purchase locally grown ingredients. Although tomatoes and ingredients from Italy may be more traditional, I do not think they will have a significant impact on the quality of the pizzas in order to justify the considerable costs of importing, which may include a tariff.

Can you think of any reasons why locally grown ingredients might be more expensive than resources that are imported from abroad?

Try to include the word 'authentic' in your paragraph and think about how this word relates to the case study.

Now try this

Write your own paragraph about Option 2 in order to complete this student's answer.

'Evaluate' questions

Worked example

Evaluate the impact on the success of The Wood Fired Pizza Company of its employees being fully qualified with the necessary food hygiene qualifications. You should use the information provided as well as your knowledge of business.

(12 marks)

Improving an answer

Having fully qualified employees means that the employees of a business will be highly skilled. For Joe's business, this is important because all of the pizzas are made by hand and this means that his employees will need the skills to do this. Having food-preparation qualifications is also very important for The Wood Fired Pizza Company because it is a fast food business that prepares food outdoors. Having these qualifications means that customers are far less likely to get food poisoning, which could have a significantly negative impact on the reputation of the company.

Having the necessary food hygiene qualifications will help reassure customers as they know the employees are properly trained, but it is not the most important consideration for most people. Customers expect the food they buy to be safe and well cooked. This means that it will do little to give the company a competitive advantage. Other factors such as the quality and taste of the food or the experience of eating freshly cooked pizza may be more important in attracting the most customers.

'Evaluate' questions

An 'evaluate' question requires a clear and well-justified conclusion based on the analysis developed in the answer. A developed evaluation may also include an 'it depends' statement, which shows consideration of other factors not mentioned in the case study.

This is just part of a student answer. It is **not** a model answer. It is a sample answer for you to improve.

The first paragraph offers a number of benefits of having employees with food hygiene qualifications. The answer is also clearly in context, referring to 'made by hand' and 'food poisoning'.

The student has failed to mention that having food hygiene qualifications might be a legal requirement of running a fast food business and that there may be legal consequences if these are not in place.

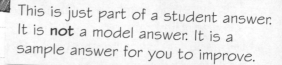 **Links** Turn to pages 36 and 37 to learn about the impact of legislation on business.

Writing a conclusion

Use the following criteria to write a conclusion. Draw a valid and well-reasoned conclusion based on a thorough evaluation of business information and issues (AO3b).

✓ Start by making a decision – is being fully qualified in food hygiene key to the success of The Wood Fired Pizza Company?

✓ Justify your decision by identifying what you think is the **most** important factor.

✓ Explain what your decision/choice may depend on.

✓ Provide The Wood Fired Pizza Company with a recommendation based on your answer, such as how they should go about implementing what you have suggested.

Now try this

 Try to include a 'depends on' statement in your conclusion to show balance.

Write a conclusion to complete the student's answer to the 'evaluate' question. Your conclusion should justify whether having food hygiene qualifications is significant. Identify what is the most important factor and anything that the justification may depend on. Try not to simply repeat the information given in the first two paragraphs.

Business growth

Once a business is established and successful, most owners want it to grow. There are different approaches to growth and you need to understand the difference between them.

Internal (organic) growth

A business grows when it sells more output over a period of time. **Business growth** is often an important objective because it may:

- help to increase market share
- lead to lower costs
- result in more profit.

Internal growth occurs when a business expands by itself, by bringing out new products or by entering new markets.

Methods of internal growth

✓ New markets – changing the marketing mix to find new markets or expanding overseas.

✓ New products – innovating (developing an existing idea or improving an existing product or service) or researching and developing brand new products that are not currently available.

✓ New technology – large organisations can benefit from investing in the latest technology or in the ability to develop new technology themselves.

External (inorganic) growth

A faster way for a business to grow is for it to join forces with another. There are two approaches to **external growth**.

- **Merger** – where two or more businesses voluntarily agree to join up and work as one business.
- **Takeover** – where one business buys another. To take over a company it is necessary to gain control by buying enough shares.

Methods of external growth

Mergers and takeovers can take place when firms join at different stages of production.

Backward vertical – business joins with one at a previous stage (e.g. a supplier)

Conglomerate – businesses with no common business interest join

Horizontal – businesses at the same stage join

Forward vertical – business joins with one at a later stage (e.g. a customer)

Worked example

State **one** reason why a business might want to grow.   (1 mark)

Higher profit

Other possible answers include to get a bigger market share, or to dominate the market. Remember that you do not need to write lots when answering 'state' questions – this student achieved one mark for stating one reason.

Now try this

Which of the following is a definition of the term 'merger'?
Select **one** answer: (1 mark)

☐ **A** Two or more businesses voluntarily join together

☐ **B** One business buys enough shares in another business to control it

☐ **C** Two businesses work together to design a new product

☐ **D** One business takes over another company

Public limited companies (PLCs)

Public limited companies (PLCs) are able to raise capital through selling shares on a **stock exchange**. This form of business ownership makes it easier for businesses to raise money for growth.

Becoming a PLC

Public limited company

30% equity in the business sold to the public through a stock exchange in order to raise share capital to finance growth

30%

70%

A private limited company (Ltd) can change into a public limited company (PLC) through a **stock market flotation**. This is where a business issues shares for sale on the stock exchange.

The benefits and drawbacks of being a PLC

👍 Ability to raise finance through share capital.

👍 Limited liability.

👍 Considered more prestigious and reliable.

👍 May be able to negotiate better prices with suppliers.

👍 Greater public awareness of business.

👎 More complex accounting and reporting procedures.

👎 Risk of potential takeovers.

👎 Increased public and media attention.

👎 Less privacy around financial performance.

👎 Greater influence on decision-making by external shareholders.

Becoming a PLC may enable a business to grow into a multinational and operate in more than one country.

Worked example

Discuss the likely benefit to a business of becoming a public limited company.   **(6 marks)**

This is just part of a student answer.

A business might become a public limited company in order to finance growth. A PLC can sell shares through a stock market, which a private limited company cannot. This means that it is able to raise capital from a wider number of potential shareholders without the risk of putting the business in debt through taking out a large loan...

When answering a 'discuss' question, you must show good understanding of business concepts and terminology. Look through this answer and highlight the key terms and concepts that the student has used in this part of their answer. This student should go on to explain a second reason for transforming into a PLC or to further develop their first point.

Now try this

Explain **one** disadvantage of becoming a public limited company.   **(3 marks)**

Financing growth

To finance growth, a business can use **internal sources of finance** from within the business or **external sources of finance** from outside the business.

Sources of finance for business growth

Internal

External

Sale of assets
A large business may have **assets** that it no longer needs, such as fixed assets (e.g. machinery) or excess stock. Selling assets is a quick way of raising capital, but the business loses the benefit of owning the assets that it sells.

Retained profit
This is the safest form of finance because it involves no risk or debt. However, profit is not guaranteed and a business may require a more substantial investment than it can make as profit.

Loan capital
A long-term bank loan can be secured against the business's assets, but interest will be charged and the business will have to make fixed repayments to repay the debt.

Share capital
A PLC can raise considerable capital by selling shares. However, selling shares puts PLCs at risk of being taken over and all shareholders are also entitled to a share of the profits through **dividends**.

Worked example

Explain **one** disadvantage to the business of borrowing money from a bank to finance growth.
(3 marks)

If a business borrows money from a bank, it has to repay the loan on a fixed-term basis with interest. A business could then struggle to make these regular payments and this could lead to cash-flow problems.

The student has identified a drawback ('repay with interest'), then given two linked strands of explanation.

Comparing sources of finance

✓ **Risk** – Selling shares may mean owners lose control, or cash-flow problems may result from meeting loan-repayment terms.

✓ **Cost** – The cost of borrowing varies across different sources.

✓ **Availability** – Some sources, such as loans or share capital, might not be accessible.

Now try this

1 State **one** internal source of finance that a business might use to expand.   **(1 mark)**
2 Explain **one** benefit to a business of using loan capital.   **(3 marks)**

Why business objectives change

As businesses evolve and grow, their objectives change, adapting to their internal needs and the external pressures of the environment. Businesses will also find that objectives need to change as they seek to grow or survive.

Factors affecting business objectives

As new **competitors** enter the market or current competitors grow and become more competitive, a business may change its objectives to become more competitive.

Objectives may be linked to the adoption of **new technology** or the innovation and invention of new products made possible by new technology.

External

Competition

Internal

Performance
Leadership
Culture

Technology

Legislation

Market conditions

Annual **objectives** reflect the previous performance of a business. A change in **working culture** or the **business's leaders** is also likely to influence its objectives so that they match the ambitions or personality of its managing director or chief executive officer (CEO).

Legislation may force a business to change its products and services. This may restrict the business's operations or create new opportunities that may be incorporated into its objectives.

The **economic climate** may change the level of demand and spending in the market. A fall or rise in demand will influence a business's ambitions and objectives.

You can revise business objectives on pages 15 and 16.

Worked example

Explain **one** reason why a business might change its objectives　**(3 marks)**

A business might change its objectives because the market conditions have changed. This may be caused by customers having less disposable income to spend. As a result, the business might decide to lower its profit objective in order to make it realistic and achievable.

Remember to develop your reasons with causes and consequences when you are answering 'explain' questions.

Now try this

Which **one** of the following is an example of an internal factor that could influence the objectives of a business?
Select **one** answer:
(1 mark)

☐ **A** Market conditions　☐ **B** Legislation　☐ **C** Culture　☐ **D** Competition

How business objectives change

Targets for a growing business

A growing business may set targets that focus on growth, such as:

- expand the product range
- enter new markets
- increase sales
- increase profits
- gain a larger market share
- take over other businesses
- open new stores
- increase the workforce.

Targets for a struggling business

A business that is struggling to survive may set targets that focus on survival, such as:

- decrease the product range
- exit markets
- achieve enough sales to break even
- improve efficiency
- maintain market share
- reduce costs, e.g. close stores or reduce the workforce.

How business objectives react to the economic climate

Business objectives

Shrinking market and negative economic climate ⟵――――――――――――――⟶ Expanding market and positive economic climate

     Retrenchment   Efficiency   Profit   Growth

Retrenchment is when a business downsizes the scale of its operations, e.g. by decreasing the range of products it sells or closing some of its stores.

Worked example

Discuss why a business might set objectives to reduce costs. **(6 marks)**

A business might set an objective to lower costs if it is facing the pressure of rising inflation, because rising inflation will increase its costs and therefore lower its profit margins. If a business can improve its efficiency, then it might be able to maintain its profits if it can keep costs low. Another reason is that a business might want to lower its prices in order to be more competitive in the market. One way to do this would be to lower costs so that prices can be reduced and profits maintained. This may work if the business operates in a competitive market that contains many similar businesses.

The student has discussed two reasons why a business might want to set an objective to reduce costs. Although both points are linked to profit, they are two different points and each is well developed.

Now try this

Explain **one** reason why a business might set an objective to increase recruitment. **(3 marks)**

Business and globalisation

Globalisation is where businesses operate internationally and gain a lot of influence or power. Globalisation changes the way businesses operate and creates considerable opportunities and threats.

The impact of globalisation

Globalisation affects businesses in three main ways.

> **Imports:** the flow of goods and services into one country from another country.
> **Exports:** the flow of goods and services out of one country to another country.

Globalisation

Imports

Globalisation allows businesses to import products and raw materials at lower prices than they would be able to produce them for in the UK, either for resale or to produce their own goods. However, importing increases competition from foreign businesses that are able to sell directly to UK customers.

Exports

Exporting opens up new international markets for businesses and gives them the potential to grow. However, operating in international markets can be very different to operating in the UK and businesses may face problems if they lack the necessary expertise or knowledge.

Location

Globalisation brings with it the opportunity for businesses to relocate operations to other countries. This may be to benefit from lower labour costs, to be closer to raw materials or to be closer to the markets to which they sell their products.

Multinationals

A multinational is a large company with facilities and markets around the world. They are powerful businesses that can create lots of jobs and growth when they enter a country. However, smaller local businesses can lose out, especially in **less economically developed countries** (LEDCs).

Benefits and drawbacks of globalisation for businesses

👍 New market opportunities.

👍 Access to technology and resources.

👎 Threat from foreign competition.

👎 Challenge of adapting products and services to meet the needs of foreign consumers.

Worked example

Explain **one** benefit of international trade for a UK business. **(3 marks)**

International trade allows UK businesses to enter new markets abroad. This means that they have a greater number of potential customers to sell to and can therefore maximise sales.

> This is a good way to answer an 'explain' question. Give one method, reason or benefit and then two linked points of development. Be careful **not** to give two separate methods, reasons or benefits if the question only asks for **one**.

Now try this

1 Define the term 'globalisation'. **(1 mark)**

2 Explain **one** drawback of globalisation for a UK company. **(3 marks)**

International trade

International trade is the exchange of goods and services between countries. **Free trade** is when there are no barriers to trade between countries. However, some governments take actions that restrict the flow of imports into their country. This is known as **protectionism**.

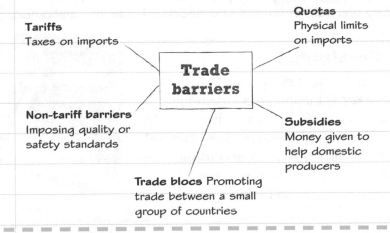

Tariffs
Taxes on imports

Quotas
Physical limits on imports

Trade barriers

Non-tariff barriers
Imposing quality or safety standards

Subsidies
Money given to help domestic producers

Trade blocs Promoting trade between a small group of countries

Reasons for trade barriers

☑ Protecting jobs in domestic industries.

☑ Protecting emerging (infant) industries.

☑ Preventing the dumping of cheap goods on the domestic market and the entry of undesirable goods.

☑ Raising revenue from tariffs.

Trade blocs

One barrier to international trade is a **trade bloc**. A trade bloc is created when the governments of different countries agree to act together to promote trade among themselves. These agreements give member nations of the trade bloc preferential treatment in other countries within the trade bloc, to encourage trade between the countries.

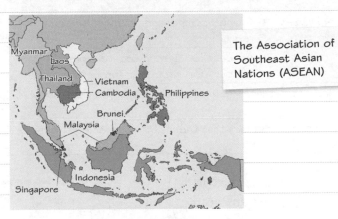

The Association of Southeast Asian Nations (ASEAN)

The North American Free Trade Association (NAFTA)

Worked example

Explain **one** trade barrier that might have an impact on a business when trading internationally. **(3 marks)**

One trade barrier is a quota. A business might be affected by a quota if the limit is reached in a country. This means that they cannot sell any more of their goods to that country and therefore sales revenues may fall.

The student has identified a relevant trade barrier and developed their answer to explain the impact this will have on a business trading internationally. Remember, there is no need to give definitions when you answer an 'explain' question.

Now try this

1 State **two** reasons for imposing trade restrictions. **(2 marks)**

2 Explain **one** drawback to a UK business of a quota placed on imports. **(3 marks)**

Competing internationally

To compete internationally, a UK business may have to adapt its products or services in order to meet the requirements of the country they are selling to and the needs of foreign customers.

E-commerce

E-commerce enables businesses to access international markets without the need to distribute or sell their products through foreign retailers. Furthermore, businesses can trade 24 hours a day when selling through e-commerce and can promote themselves through social media sites. However, trade barriers may still apply when selling over the internet.

Glocalisation

In order to sell to international markets, businesses often have to change their products in order to adapt to other countries' cultural differences, tastes and legal requirements. This strategy is known as **glocalisation**.

Customers in different countries have different needs. For example, in India consuming beef is illegal in many states, so a Maharaja Mac is made from chicken instead.

How businesses change their marketing mix to compete internationally

Element	Strategy	
Product	• Change technological components (e.g. sockets) • Change taste to meet cultural preferences	• Change components to meet safety regulations
Price	• Change price to consider tariffs • Comply with different tax laws	• Account for currency conversions • Account for incomes in foreign countries
Place	• Change location of products in line with local preferences (e.g. which shops people visit and what time they shop)	
Promotion	• Revise advertising campaigns to take into account the fact that the meanings of colours, gestures and phrases are different in different countries	

Worked example

This is just part of a student answer.

Discuss how a business might change its products or services in order to compete in international markets. **(6 marks)**

A business might change its products to compete internationally by changing the features of the product so that it meets the legal requirements of other countries, e.g. adapting electrical components so that they are compatible abroad. There may also be legal requirements for health and safety that a business is required to meet, such as providing certain information on a label. Providing this information would ensure that the business was able to meet safety standards for that country. This would mean more distributors and retailers would be willing to stock their products as they would know they are safe.

The student has identified a relevant method ('to meet legal requirements') and has given two good examples. Examples are a useful way of illustrating your point. This answer requires more development and analysis to explain how this will help the business compete.

Now try this

Explain **one** benefit to a business of changing its product in order to compete internationally. **(3 marks)**

Ethics and business

Ethics are the moral principles that guide the behaviours of individuals and businesses. When making decisions, businesses must consider the impact they have on all stakeholders.

Profits or ethics?

A **trade-off** is when something is given up in order to gain or achieve something else. Businesses must balance the drive for profit with their ethical principles.

Paying higher wages and using ethical suppliers is likely to raise costs and lower profits. However, acting ethically can appeal to customers and motivate staff, leading to higher productivity and more sales.

Is paying the minimum wage fair?

Is it right to collaborate with competitors to keep prices high?

How much waste should a business produce and how should it dispose of waste safely?

Pressure groups

Pressure groups are organisations that try to make businesses change their behaviour or operations. Pressure groups focus on issues such as animal rights, workers' rights, the environment and world poverty. Pressure groups can cause bad publicity for businesses that act unethically, which can damage the businesses' reputations.

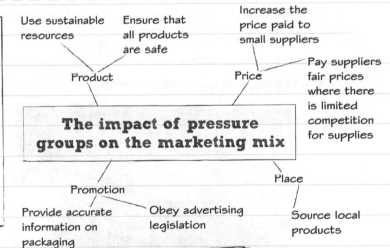

Use sustainable resources

Ensure that all products are safe

Increase the price paid to small suppliers

Product

Price

Pay suppliers fair prices where there is limited competition for supplies

The impact of pressure groups on the marketing mix

Promotion

Place

Provide accurate information on packaging

Obey advertising legislation

Source local products

Examples of ethical behaviour by businesses

- ✓ Treating workers and suppliers fairly.
- ✓ Being honest with customers.
- ✓ Ethical sourcing of materials.
- ✓ Investing in the community.
- ✓ Meeting government requirements and legislation.
- ✓ Caring for the environment and operating sustainably.

Worked example

Which **two** of the following are **not** examples of ethical behaviour by a business?   **(2 marks)**

Select **two** answers:

- ☐ **A** Paying employees a fair wage
- ☒ **B** Paying a low price to suppliers
- ☐ **C** Placing full details of product content on packaging
- ☐ **D** Carefully disposing of waste
- ☒ **E** Using non-renewable resources

Paying suppliers a low price is unethical if the suppliers have no choice but to accept the price. Non renewable resources cannot be replenished so their use is not sustainable.

Now try this

1 Give **one** method a pressure group could use to persuade a business to act responsibly.   **(1 mark)**

2 Explain **one** disadvantage to a business of being ethical.   **(3 marks)**

Environmental issues

Most business operations will have short-term and long-term impacts on the environment. All businesses have to minimise any negative impact that they have in order to achieve long-term success.

Impact on the environment

Short-term impacts	Long-term impacts
Traffic congestion through transport and deliveries	Climate change
Air, noise and water pollution through manufacturing and industry	Depletion of land, food and natural resources

The environmental impact of a business is closely linked to its growth. As businesses expand, they will normally have a bigger impact on the environment.

Reducing the impact

Recycling is one way of reducing the environmental impact of business. Other ways include:

- ✓ using renewable energy
- ✓ replenishing and conserving natural resources
- ✓ using biodegradable packaging
- ✓ reducing food miles
- ✓ partaking in social enterprises.

Help the environment! Recycle office waste paper

Business opportunities

As consumers are becoming more environmentally aware, there is an opportunity for businesses to differentiate their products to meet customer needs and make them 'greener', e.g. the development of hybrid cars. There are also growing opportunities for businesses in 'green' industries, such as energy conservation and solar power.

Many businesses have set up recycling schemes. Waste paper is collected and recycled for other uses.

Worked example

Explain **one** way a business might limit its impact on the environment.

(3 marks)

One way that a business might limit its impact on the environment is by minimising the amount of waste it produces. This means that less waste is going into landfill sites, which ensures that there is less polluting of the natural environment.

The student has identified a relevant way and developed two points explaining how this approach will reduce the negative impact on the environment. The student used specific examples ('landfill sites').

Now try this

Give **two** impacts a business might have on the environment.

(2 marks)

Product 1

The variables that contribute to a successful design are function, cost and appearance. In order for a business to successfully achieve this **design mix**, it may carry out scientific research and development.

The design mix of a product can **differentiate** it from other products. For a laptop, the design mix may include the following.

- **Function** – This is about how well a product does what it is meant to. For a laptop, this would include processing speed, memory and performance of the software.

- **Cost** – The cost is closely linked to price. Businesses will try to keep costs low, but improved functionality and appearance will increase cost. The better the technology and screen size, the more expensive the laptop will cost to produce.

- **Appearance** – Style and elegance are important for many products. Modern laptops can be found in multiple colours and continue to be designed to be thinner and lighter.

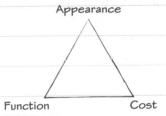

Appearance

Function   Cost

Businesses must find the right design mix in order to make products that are desirable and profitable.

The product life cycle

The product is launched / released onto the market.

If the launch is successful sales increase sharply and the product may make a profit for the first time.

Sales growth slows down, but repeat customers continue to buy and customers become loyal. The market becomes saturated as rivals bring out competing products.

Eventually the product is outdated and there is a big fall in sales, leading to withdrawal.

SALES | Introduction | Growth | Maturity | Decline

SALES

TIME

What promotion methods will encourage customers to trial a product?

How can we meet demand and maintain customer service?

How can we encourage repeat purchase and build customer loyalty?

How can we innovate products to compete with competitors? Should we use extension strategies?

Define the term 'product life cycle'. **(1 mark)**

The product life cycle is a business model that represents the sales of a product through different stages of its life.

A definition sentence should be short and to the point, normally giving two specific points.

Now try this

Explain **one** benefit to a business of balancing its product's design mix. **(3 marks)**

Product 2

Extension strategies

Businesses can increase the life of a product using **extension strategies**. This involves slightly changing the product so that it has a fresh appeal to the target market or appeals to a new market segment.

Think about how the product life cycle links all aspects of marketing together.

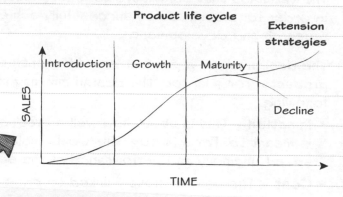

Product life cycle

Extension strategies could include a new marketing campaign, a modified product or a change of packaging – anything that will create new interest and boost sales.

Product differentiation

Product differentiation is about making a product different from other products in some way. It is important because it helps businesses:

- to position their products and target different market segments
- to gain an advantage over rivals when faced with competition.

It allows consumers to see clearly that their needs are being met more effectively by one product than by another.

Differentiating a product

- ✓ Unique and catchy product name
- ✓ Quality
- ✓ Design, formulation or function
- ✓ Packaging
- ✓ Customer service
- ✓ Differentiation across the value chain

Worked example

Discuss the benefit to a business of differentiating its products and services.

(6 marks)

If a business can differentiate its products, then it may be able to create a unique selling point (USP). If the business has a USP, it will stand out from its competitors and may be more attractive to potential customers. When products are unique, certain customers may also find them more desirable or specific to their needs. If a product meets the needs of a specific market segment, then these customers might be happy to pay a premium price for them.

A 'discuss' question can be answered by discussing one issue, with five or more strands of discussion developed from one or two points, each with some development and explanation.

Now try this

Give **two** methods that a business could use to differentiate its brand.

(2 marks)

The importance of price

Price is a key part of the marketing mix. The pricing strategy adopted by a business has a direct impact on customers' perceptions of quality and value, the business's profitability and the demand for products and services.

The importance of price in the marketing mix

- The price of a product gives customers an indication of quality.

- In competitive markets, changes in price can have a significant influence on demand.

- Branded products generally have a higher price than non-branded products because they are more expensive to produce and promote.

Different types of price

Luxury brands can charge a **premium price** for their products.

Many pricing decisions are based on comparing the average market price – what other businesses charge for their products and services. This is known as **competitor pricing**.

A low price might be used by **generic/non-branded products** or to encourage **product trial** when a product is first launched.

Quantitative skills **Price and profit**

A business may try to improve its profits by increasing the price of its products and services. If this strategy is to succeed, customers must perceive the business's products and services to be of sufficiently high value in relation to competitors' products. If they do not, the business may find that its sales volume falls.

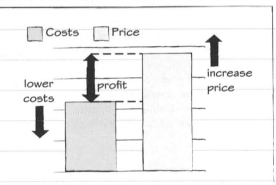

Worked example

Explain **one** reason why a business might lower its prices. **(3 marks)**

A business might lower its prices in order to sell off unwanted stock. If its prices fall, this would mean that their products would be more desirable and customers may be willing to purchase more, leading to a higher sales volume.

The student has given a valid reason and clearly explained why this might work.

Now try this

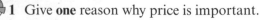

1 Give **one** reason why price is important. **(1 mark)**

2 Give **one** reason why a business might set a premium price for its products. **(1 mark)**

Pricing strategies

A business may adopt a volume strategy or a margin strategy. A **margin strategy** involves setting a price that achieves a high profit margin. A **volume strategy** involves setting a price with a low profit margin, which requires high sales volumes in order to be profitable.

Volume and margin strategies

The choice of pricing strategy will often depend on the nature of the product and the quantity of the product that a business intends to sell.

A business with a high volume low margin strategy must be able to keep costs low and have the facilities to produce and distribute large quantities.

A business can adopt a pricing strategy anywhere between these two extremes.

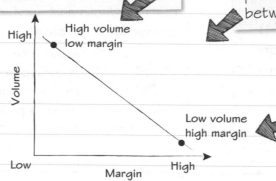

A low volume high margin strategy might be determined by the quality of the product and its brand image. Businesses using this strategy will target the premium end of the market.

Competition – a business has to consider its competitors and the position of its brand in the market

Technology – new technology can lower the costs of production and allow a business to set a more competitive price

Market segment – different prices may be applied to customers with different characteristics

Branding – products with a strong brand can demand a higher price due to the perceived value and desirability

Influences on pricing strategy

Product life cycle – the product's stage in the product life cycle will influence pricing decisions

Costs – a business may set itself a profit margin target (e.g. 150%) that it adds to the cost of the product or service in order to set its price

Worked example

Explain **one** method a business might use to increase its profits.

(3 marks)

A business could increase its advertising. This could lead to greater awareness and interest in its products and therefore more revenue through sales.

This is a good answer. Another way to approach this question would be to explain how changing the pricing strategy could lead to increased sales revenue. The student could have referred to a volume or a margin strategy.

Now try this

Discuss why a business might only need to sell low volumes of its products in order to be profitable. **(6 marks)**

Promotion

Businesses use **promotion** techniques to create customer awareness of, interest in and desire for their products. Effective promotion will also allow a business to build a strong brand image and help boost sales at various times.

Features of promotion methods

Method	Examples	Benefits	Drawbacks
Advertising	TV, radio, magazines, posters, websites, point-of-sales displays, leaflets and brochures	👍 Can have a big impact and grab customers' attention if the advert is in the right place and uses the right medium	👎 Can be expensive and it can also be difficult to work out the impact of advertising on sales
Sponsorship	Sponsoring sporting events, music festivals and good causes such as educational or environmental causes	👍 Can provide a business with a lot of exposure and associate it with a good cause	👎 Communicates very little information about the features and benefits of products and services
Product trials	Free miniatures, product testing and samples given away with other products	👍 Can encourage customers to use a new product or service that they might not try otherwise	👎 Can be expensive to give away free products
Special offers	Buy one get one free (BOGOF), free prize draws and discount sales	👍 Can boost short-term sales and clear stock levels	👎 Not sustainable in the long term as selling at a discount will reduce profits
Public relations You can revise branding in more detail on page 64.	Using a recognisable logo on all promotional materials so that customers remember it and associate it with the product/ business	👍 Can encourage customers to connect with the brand, trust it and become loyal to it	👎 Takes a long time to develop a strong brand and brand image can be damaged quickly by bad publicity

The choice of promotion technique or medium will depend on the characteristics of the market segment being targeted (the target market).

Worked example

This is just part of a student answer.

Discuss the likely benefit to a business of carrying out extensive promotion. **(6 marks)**

Carrying out extensive promotion will benefit a business because people will become far more aware of it and its products. This awareness could lead to customers choosing the business over other competitors. Consumers are more likely to purchase and trust a brand that they have heard of over a brand that they have not heard of before...

The student has started their answer by identifying a relevant benefit. They have then gone on to link their answer to how promotion can lead to a strong brand image and the benefits that this might have. Next, the student could go on to explain the link between promotion and increased sales revenue.

Now try this

Explain **one** benefit to a business of using product trials to promote new products. **(3 marks)**

Promotion, branding and technology

Branding

A **brand** is more than a logo or a slogan. Although customers will remember a business's logo and slogan, a brand also represents the characteristics and personality of a business. For example, customers may associate a brand with characteristics such as 'sophistication', 'fun', 'value for money' or 'premium quality'. A strong brand can be created by investing in successful promotion.

The value of a strong brand

A business may benefit from a strong brand in many ways:

- customers may instantly recognise the brand and what it represents
- customers may associate positive characteristics with the brand
- a well-known brand may become a first choice for customers, increasing **brand loyalty**
- customers may trust a strong brand
- a strong brand may allow a business to charge a premium for their products and services.

Social media – a cheap form of communication that provides opportunities for viral advertising

Apps – businesses' apps for consumers and the opportunity to advertise through third-party apps

Technology in promotion

Email – communications such as e-newsletters that can be tailored to the needs and interests of customers

Targeted advertising – website adverts that use **cookies** and are targeted at particular consumers or market segments

Through technology, businesses are able to reach a wider variety of customers at a lower cost than most traditional forms of promotion. Some forms of technology also allow businesses to deliver a personal message specific to individual customers.

Worked example

Explain **one** reason why a business may want to develop a strong brand.

(3 marks)

A business may want a strong brand because customers trust brands that they recognise and are familiar with. This means that customers may be willing to buy from the brand without needing additional reassurance about a product's quality and features. As a result, a business with a strong brand can expect to achieve more sales.

> Make sure you know what a brand is and the benefits of a strong brand. A strong brand is one that many consumers recognise and have positive associations with – i.e. they trust it.

Now try this

1 Define the term 'viral advertising'. **(1 mark)**

2 Explain **one** reason why a business may choose to launch its own smartphone app. **(3 marks)**

Place

Place is about making products and services available to customers when and where those customers want them. There are a number of channels that a business can use to make it easy for customers to access their products and services.

Channels of distribution

1 Retailing:

Manufacturer   Retailer   Customer

2 Retailing:

Retailer   Customer

3 E-tailing:

Manufacturer   Customer

4 E-tailing:

Manufacturer   Third party e-tailer   Customer

Benefits of retailing

- Customers have the opportunity to browse and try products.
- Retailing offers point-of-sale promotion (e.g. displays).
- Retailers can provide customers with help and advice.
- Many customers enjoy the experience of shopping in a retail store.

Benefits of e-tailing

- Businesses do not have to rent or own expensive retail space.
- Customers can buy at any time of any day.
- Businesses can access customers around the world.
- Small businesses are able to compete with larger businesses without needing retail space.

Location

When choosing a site at which to locate a retail store, a business must consider:

- cost
- proximity to competitors
- proximity to the labour market
- proximity to resources and transport links.

The importance of each factor will vary for different businesses.

Explain **one** reason why place is an important aspect of the marketing mix.

(3 marks)

If a business gets 'place' right they will make their products more accessible to customers. As a result it is likely that there will be greater customer awareness, which could lead to increased sales over time.

When answering this question, the student could have made reference to either retailing or e-tailing.

Now try this

Which **one** of the following elements of the marketing mix does 'online' represent?

Select **one** answer:

(1 mark)

- ☐ **A** Price
- ☐ **B** Product
- ☐ **C** Promotion
- ☐ **D** Place

Integrated marketing mix

The marketing mix consists of four different elements, but these elements should combine to form one joined-up or **integrated** marketing strategy that the business uses to meet the needs its customers' needs.

Linking the 4 Ps

If one aspect of the marketing mix does not link up with the others, it is highly likely that the business's marketing strategy will fail.

Increasing the features and function of a **product** will have a direct impact on the business's **pricing** strategy.

A **product** targeted at a premium market must be **promoted** using appropriate channels (e.g. magazines or online) to ensure that the message reaches its target audience

Different **products** can be sold in different **places**, as some are more suited to e-tailing while others require the experience and customer service provided by retailers.

If a business uses a high volume low margin **pricing** strategy, it is likely that there will be very little budget available for **promotion**.

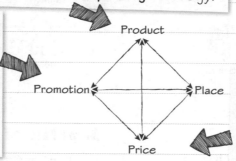

The marketing mix and competitive advantage

An effective marketing mix can help a business build a **competitive advantage** over its rivals.

A competitive advantage is an advantage that one business has over a competitor. The advantage is unique and difficult to copy.

- Product – a product with unique features and a strong brand can be highly desirable.
- Price – a business that finds a way to set its prices lower than its competitors' will be more competitive.
- Promotion – a successful advertising campaign can attract consumers' attention and build a unique brand.
- Place – a highly visible and convenient business location can help a business attract customers that other competitors cannot attract.

When reading a business case study, always consider which 'P' might be the most important for the success of the business in question. For example, in a highly competitive market where products are very similar, price may be the most important element of the marketing mix.

Business operations and production

Operations is the business function that organises, produces and delivers the goods and services produced or provided by a business. It is the key function that transforms resources into finished goods (a physical product) and services (a solution or utility).

The production process

The production process involves a business using its resources (e.g. raw materials, finance and the skills and knowledge of its workforce) to produce goods and provide services that customers can buy.

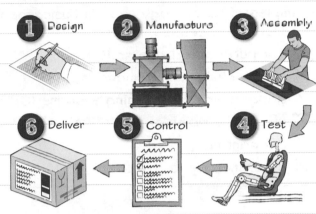

1 Design   2 Manufacture   3 Assembly

6 Deliver   5 Control   4 Test

Production methods

A business may use one of three different production methods. The choice of method will depend on the nature of the product and the level of production.

Job production	Batch production	Flow production
E.g. a house extension	E.g. a batch of cupcakes	E.g. a mass-produced laptop
• One-off or **bespoke** products • Focus on customer needs and individual service • Specialist skilled workforce increases costs • High profit margins • Longer production process	• Larger volume of products than job production • Some flexibility (e.g. different flavours) • Semi-skilled workforce • Some levels of automation • Productivity reduced when switching between batches	• High volumes and low margins (with high productivity) • Standardised production • Low skilled workforce • Highly automated process • Setting up expensive machinery increases costs

Production and competitive advantage

Operations is linked to productivity, flexibility, cost and quality. For example, if a business can provide custom products and services, this will make their products more desirable to customers. Similarly, controlling production costs can allow a business to lower prices or increase profit margins. You can revise the definition of productivity on page 68.

Worked example

Explain **one** benefit to a business of improving its productivity. **(3 marks)**

If a business improves its productivity, it will have more products to sell that are produced at a lower cost. This means the business can improve its profit margins and will have more products to sell to its customers.

The student has made the connection between productivity, costs and profit.

Now try this

Define the term 'job production'. **(1 mark)**

Business operations and technology

Technology used in business operations

Examples of technology used in businesses' production processes include:

- ✓ computer-aided design (CAD)
- ✓ supply chain management (SCM)
- ✓ geographical positioning systems (GPS)
- ✓ electronic point of sale (EPoS)
- ✓ 3D printing
- ✓ e-commerce.

The impact of technology on operations

- 👍 Speeds up the production process.
- 👍 Keeps businesses in touch with their customers.
- 👍 Lowers production costs.
- 👍 Ensures fewer mistakes and defects.
- 👎 Can involve a costly initial investment.
- 👎 Can quickly become obsolete.
- 👎 Requires employees to be trained to use new technology.

Economies of scale

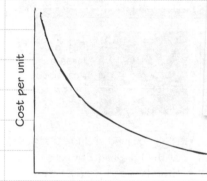

Economies of scale is a term that describes the situation where the average costs of production fall as the volume of production increases. This is an advantage that businesses gain as they grow in size.

Productivity

Productivity is output per worker. It measures how much each worker produces over a period of time.

Increasing productivity leads to greater competitiveness in a market. Productivity can be improved by increasing output or by lowering the costs of production (inputs) while maintaining output.

Factors influencing the use of technology

There are several factors that need to be considered when a business adopts the use of technology in its operations. Technology can have an impact on each of these factors and they all need to be balanced. For example, a technology that improves productivity may have a negative impact on quality.

Productivity   Cost

Factors affecting choice of technology

Flexibility   Quality

Discuss how investment in technology can help improve the productivity of a business. **(6 marks)**

One way that technology can help improve productivity is by speeding up the production process. Many businesses use robotics and computer-aided manufacturing to make their products. Although this can be more expensive, a computer-operated machine can produce more products than a human can and with fewer errors...

The student has used a good example to illustrate their point. How would you finish this answer?

This is just part of a student answer.

Give **two** methods a business could use to reduce costs in the production process. **(2 marks)**

Managing stock

Managing stock is about managing the materials that a business holds in the most efficient and effective way. Stock can include materials waiting to be used in the production process, work in progress, and some can be finished stock waiting to be delivered to customers.

Interpreting bar gate stock graphs

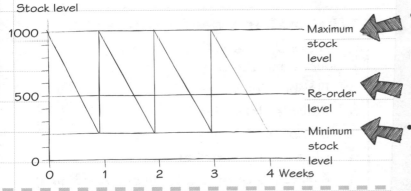

- The **maximum stock level** is the most stock that a business can hold.
- The **re-order level** is the level of stock at which new stock will be ordered by the business. The difference between this level and the point at which stock increases is the time it takes for the stock to arrive.
- Also known as **buffer stock**, the **minimum stock level** is the lowest amount of stock the business will hold. It is a safety net in case there is a surge in demand.

Just in time stock control

Just in time (JIT) stock control is a stock management system where stock is delivered only when it is needed by the production system, and so no stock is kept by a business. For JIT to work, a business must have good relationships with suppliers, a well-organised production system, and regular demand for their products.

Holding stock

Benefits of holding stock:

- ☑ Any unpredicted surges in demand can be met.
- ☑ Damaged goods can be replaced.
- ☑ Businesses can receive discounts for bulk buying.
- ☑ Limited risk of problems supplying customer demand.

Benefits of holding little or no stock:

- ☑ Cost saving in not having to store stock.
- ☑ Less chance of damaged or stolen stock.
- ☑ Employees can focus on tasks other than managing stock.
- ☑ Can reduce costs of production, which makes product pricing more competitive.

Worked example

The diagram illustrates the bar gate stock for Movin' Mice at the Chipping Toy Box.

Using the diagram, calculate how many weeks it will take for stock of Movin' Mice to arrive at the Chipping Toy Box after re-ordering. You are advised to show your workings. **(2 marks)**

Stock is ordered in week 3 and arrives in week 8. Therefore 8 − 3 = 5 weeks.

Always show workings when answering a 'calculate' question.

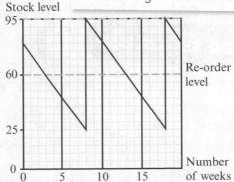

Now try this

Using the diagram in the worked example, identify the number of Movin' Mice the Chipping Toy Box holds as a buffer stock.

(1 mark)

Suppliers and procurement

Choosing the right supplier to work with is an important decision for a business. Suppliers can have a significant impact on a business's costs, flexibility, reliability and customer relations.

Working with suppliers

A business may use one supplier or many suppliers. Suppliers are a key part of a business's operation and finding the right supplier could be crucial to a business's competitiveness and success. Businesses may consider several different factors when choosing a supplier. One factor may be more important than others due to the nature of the products and the business.

What makes a good supplier?

- ✓ A good price (value for money) on products and delivery
- ✓ Flexible deliveries
- ✓ Reliable deliveries
- ✓ Discounts for large orders
- ✓ High-quality supplies
- ✓ Availability of products (short lead times)

The impact of logistics and suppliers

Suppliers and logistics can have a significant impact on the operations of a business. A business needs a supplier they can trust.

Flexible suppliers can help a business meet customer needs more easily.

Late deliveries can hold up production.

Poor quality can lead to dissatisfied customers and products being returned.

 Supplier

Business

Customers

The services provided by a supplier can directly influence the reputation of the business that uses its products.

Securing good contracts and supplier agreements can help a business achieve economies of scale as it grows.

Using a supplier to deliver products directly to customers can be risky if they are not reliable.

Explain **one** reason why a good supplier relationship is important for a business.   **(3 marks)**

A good supplier relationship could ensure that the supplier is willing to be flexible. This might mean that the business is able to change orders at short notice and get raw materials and products delivered quickly. As a result, the business will be better equipped to meet its customers' needs.

The student has made a connection between a good supplier relationship and the impact this could have on the ability of the business to satisfy its customers.

Now try this

 1 Define the term 'stock'.   **(1 mark)**

2 Explain **one** factor that a business may consider when choosing a supplier.   **(3 marks)**

Managing quality

There are two ways of achieving good quality in business: **quality control** and **quality assurance**.

- **Quality control** is seen as one part of the chain of production. A quality controller will examine and/or test for quality once a product has been made or a service has been delivered.

- **Quality assurance** involves focusing on quality at every stage of the production process. Everyone is involved and is responsible for contributing to the achievement of a quality standard. As a result, there should be zero defects.

The benefits of good quality

☑ Good quality allows for a premium price to be charged.

☑ Good quality builds a strong brand image.

☑ Good quality is closely linked to meeting customer needs and can help provide a competitive advantage.

☑ Quality is a way of differentiating a product.

Quality also ensures that there is less waste because there are fewer faulty products, which helps businesses to control their costs.

Quality assurance checklist

A quality assurance system requires a business to:

☑ have quality as the focus of every process

☑ involve customers and suppliers at the design stage

☑ aim for zero defects

☑ have quality as the responsibility of every employee

☑ have managers who ensure there are systems in place to assure quality

☑ meet a **quality standard**, such as **ISO 9000**

☑ make good quality part of the business's culture, so it is something everyone aims for and is involved in.

Worked example

This is just part of a student's answer.

Discuss the reasons why a business may choose to adopt quality assurance in the production process. **(6 marks)**

A business might choose to use quality assurance because it ensures that every employee takes responsibility for the quality of the products and services they produce, instead of a small number of quality control officers. Consequently, there will be a lower proportion of faulty products and customers who are dissatisfied with the service they receive. This will help a business build a solid reputation for quality and avoid the costs associated with repairing or replacing faulty goods...

The student has identified a reason for using quality assurance. They have then gone on to develop their answer with multiple strands of reasoning to explain the benefits the business might receive. The student could now go on to explain a second point, with several more linked strands of development.

Now try this

Explain **one** benefit to a business of producing high-quality products.

(3 marks)

Customer service and the sales process

Many customers place the greatest value on the customer service they receive from a business, even more than the price they pay or the quality of the product. Customer service is one way that a business can add value to its products and services.

The importance of customer service

Good customer service leads to:

👍 satisfied and loyal customers

👍 positive brand image and reputation

👍 differentiated products with a competitive advantage

👍 increased sales and repeat purchasing.

Poor customer service leads to:

👎 poor customer satisfaction and low customer loyalty

👎 poor brand image

👎 inability to differentiate products and to charge premium prices

👎 falling sales and repeat purchases.

The sales process

The sales process identifies the key stages of buying a product or service that contribute to customer satisfaction. This means that it is an important part of providing excellent customer service.

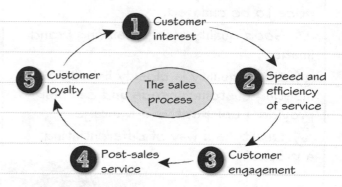

Factors affecting the sales process

Some products have a short sales process (e.g. a bar of chocolate), while others may involve an extended sales process over a number of months (e.g. a house purchase). A business needs to manage each stage of the process effectively to ensure the sale is complete and customers are totally satisfied.

Depending on the product or service being sold, the business may need to consider:

• the product knowledge of its sales staff

• the speed and efficiency of its service

• customer engagement with its products

• its responses to customer feedback

• the post-sales service that it provides.

Considering the sales process

Businesses may consider these questions about the five stages of the sales process.

1 How can we grab the attention and interest of potential customers? (e.g. using emotive language in advertising)

2 How can we ensure that we respond to customers' needs promptly? (e.g. ensuring all customers receive a call back within 1 hour)

3 How can we build relationships with customers and meet their needs? (e.g. having regular communication with customers and inviting them to special events)

4 How can we ensure that customers remain happy after buying our products? (e.g. using follow-up surveys to measure satisfaction levels)

5 How can we encourage customers to continue to buy and engage with our brand? (e.g. making customers aware of new product launches)

Now try this

Give **two** drawbacks to a business of poor customer service. **(2 marks)**

Gross and net profit

When managing the finances of a business, it is useful to distinguish between two specific measures of profit – **gross profit** and **net profit**. You may want to revisit profit on page 18 before you revise gross profit and net profit on this page.

Calculating gross profit and net profit

Income Statement: Year 1	
Sales (Revenue)	
Celebration cakes	8979.00
Cakes stocked in store	2742.00
Cafe cakes	6379.00
Total sales	**18100.00**
Cost of sales:	
Materials and ingredients	3218.00
Gross profit	**14882.00**
Expenses (Costs)	
Interest on bank loan	240.00
Rent, business rates etc.	1620.00
Salaries	7400.00
Equipment & repairs	3317.00
Electricity, water etc.	743.00
Total expenses	**13320.00**
Net income (profit/loss)	**(1562.00)**

A profit and loss account for ABC Trading Ltd

Quantitative skills

Gross profit is the profit that a business makes on its trading activity before any indirect costs have been deducted. **LEARN IT!**

Gross profit = Sales revenue − Cost of sales
(or turnover)   (the cost of buying, producing and distributing products and services)

Quantitative skills

Net profit (also known as the bottom line) is the profit that a business is able to return to shareholders (owners) or reinvest back into the business. **LEARN IT!**

Net profit = Gross profit − Other operating expenses and interest

Improving profit

A business can **improve profit** by lowering costs or increasing revenue. However, this can cause problems.

- The problem with increasing revenue is that the methods used can also increase costs.

- The problem with lowering costs is that doing so can detract from the value of the product or service, reducing the business's ability to make revenue.

Lowering costs and increasing revenue are two ways of improving profit.

Worked example

Using the profit and loss account for ABC Trading Ltd above, calculate gross profit.   **(2 marks)**

Total sales	−	Cost of sales (direct costs)	=	Gross profit
£18100	−	£3218	=	**£14882**

LEARN IT!

Quantitative skills The student has clearly shown the steps they have taken to calculate the gross profit, starting with the formula. The direct costs in this example are the materials and ingredients of the cakes.

Now try this

Explain **one** reason a business might calculate its gross profit.   **(3 marks)**

73

Profit margins and ARR

A **profit margin** is the ratio of profit compared to sales revenue. Businesses will calculate the **gross profit margin (GPM)** and the **net profit margin (NPM)** of their products and services. Profit margins give an indication of a product's profitability.

Income Statement: Year 1	
Sales (Revenue)	
Celebration cakes	8979.00
Cakes stocked in store	2742.00
Cafe cakes	6379.00
Total sales	**18100.00**
Cost of sales:	
Materials and ingredients	3218.00
Gross profit	**14882.00**
Expenses (Costs)	
Interest on bank loan	240.00
Rent, business rates etc.	1620.00
Salaries	7400.00
Equipment & repairs	3317.00
Electricity, water etc.	743.00
Total expenses	**13320.00**
Net income (profit/loss)	**(1562.00)**

Quantitative skills

The GPM indicates the proportion of sales revenue turned into gross profit. For example, a 40% GPM indicates that 40p in every £1 of sales becomes gross profit.

$$\text{Gross profit margin (\%)} = \frac{\text{Gross profit}}{\text{Sales revenue}} \times 100$$

LEARN IT!

Quantitative skills

The NPM indicates the proportion of sales revenue turned into net profit. For example, an 8% NPM indicates that 8p in every £1 of sales becomes net profit.

$$\text{Net profit margin (\%)} = \frac{\text{Net profit}}{\text{Sales revenue}} \times 100$$

LEARN IT!

Quantitative skills   **Average rate of return (ARR)**   **LEARN IT!**

$$\text{Average rate of return (\%)} = \frac{\text{Average annual profit (Total profit / No. of years)}}{\text{Cost of investment}} \times 100$$

A business will calculate the average return that it receives on an investment over the investment's life span as a percentage of the initial cost of the investment. The calculation is used to compare different investment opportunities to identify which is the most profitable.

Year	Net cash flow (£)	
	Option A: New machinery	Option B: Extend factory
0	(£600 000)	(£1 000 000)
1	£200 000	£300 000
2	£300 000	£300 000
3	£200 000	£300 000
4	£100 000	£300 000

Table 1: Investment opportunities for ABC Trading Ltd

A number shown in brackets is negative, or a cash outflow.

Worked example

Using the information in Table 1, calculate the average rate of return for Option A.   **(2 marks)**

$$\text{Average annual profit} = \frac{(200\,000 + 300\,000 + 200\,000 + 100\,000)}{4} = £200\,000$$

$$\text{Average rate of return} = \frac{\text{Average annual profit (Total profit / No. of years)}}{\text{Cost of investment}} \times 100$$

$$\text{Average rate of return} = \frac{200\,000}{600\,000} \times 100$$

$$\text{Average rate of return} = 0.3333 \times 100 = \textbf{33.3\%}$$

Quantitative skills

An ARR of 33.3% suggests that, on average, this project gains a return of 33.3% each year based on the initial investment of £600 000.

Now try this

Define the term 'average rate of return'.   **(1 mark)**

Interpreting quantitative business data

Businesses use **quantitative data** from a wide variety of sources to make informed business decisions. The accuracy and reliability of this data is extremely important in order to help businesses make the right decisions. You can revise the use of data in market research on page 10.

Uses of data

A business will use quantitative data to:

- monitor the performance of the business
- compare its performance with that of its competitors
- anticipate the needs of customers or identify trends in the market
- make business decisions, e.g. production volume and sales targets
- set business aims and objectives.

Graphs and charts

Graphs and charts can be created using quantitative data to:

- demonstrate the relationships or **correlation** between two sets of data
- represent proportions (percentages)
- show trends over time and make forecasts
- measure the performance of a business
- identify unusual factors or events, and their impact on the business.

Quantitative skills

Interpreting graphs and charts

Make sure you understand what the axes represent. Consider whether the graph or chart shows any of the factors listed above.

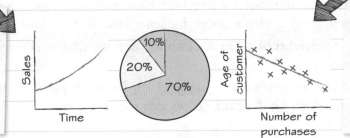

A **graph** is a visual representation of business data.
A **chart** is a very easy-to-interpret visual representation (e.g. a pie chart) that shows differences in information.

Worked example

The chart shows the sales volumes for a business during its first three months of trading. The selling price of its product is £250.

Calculate the business's revenue for the first three months of trading. **(2 marks)**

Revenue = Price × Quantity **LEARN IT!**

Jan revenue = 4000 × 250 = 1000000

Feb revenue = 5000 × 250 = 1250000

Mar revenue = 2500 × 250 = 625000

Total revenue for first three months = £2875000

Quantitative skills

Be prepared to read financial data from tables and charts in your exam.

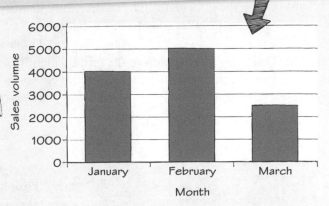

Now try this

Explain **one** way that a business might use its historical sales revenue figures. **(3 marks)**

Limitations of quantitative data

Quantitative data is information that can be expressed in numbers, such as percentages, ratios, profits and indices. Financial data is a particularly important type of quantitative data used in business.

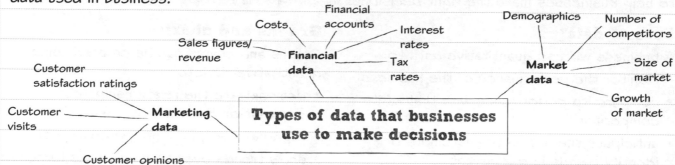

Costs

Financial accounts

Interest rates

Sales figures/revenue

Financial data

Tax rates

Demographics

Number of competitors

Market data

Size of market

Growth of market

Customer satisfaction ratings

Customer visits

Marketing data

Customer opinions

Types of data that businesses use to make decisions

The limitations of financial data

There are several limitations of financial data that businesses need to consider when making decisions that are based on financial information.

- It is **historical** – when using financial data, businesses will make decisions about the future based on past performance.

- The **reasons** behind the numbers – the fact that sales revenue has fallen might not be as important as understanding the market factors that led to the fall in revenue.

- Statistics can be **manipulated** – facts can be expressed in different ways to give them a different emphasis.

- Business performance is **not solely judged** on financial performance – there are many other **qualitative** factors that need to be considered, e.g. business reputation and employee motivation.

Worked example

The diagrams show data on smoothie consumption.

(a) Using the information in the diagrams, identify the most popular time to buy a smoothie.

(1 mark)

(b) Using the information in the graphs, identify how the majority of people prefer to consume a smoothie.

(1 mark)

(a) After lunch (1 to 5 p.m.)

(b) As a snack (59%)

Smoothie sales throughout the day

14% After 5 p.m.

15% Before 11 a.m.

41% After lunch (1 to 5 p.m.)

30% During lunch rush (11 a.m. to 1 p.m.)

Smoothies: a snack or a meal?

59% Snack

25% Part of a meal

16% Meal

Quantitative skills

'Identify' questions require you to interpret information from a graph, chart or diagram. Make sure you practise reading these.

Now try this

Discuss the reasons why a business should be cautious when using financial data to make business decisions.

(6 marks)

Organisational structures

Organisational structure is the way in which a business is structured to achieve its objectives. This is normally through a **hierarchy**. A hierarchy is a structure of different levels of authority in a business organisation, one on top of the other.

Hierarchical and flat structures

A business with a **hierarchical structure** has a long chain of command. This makes the business easier to control and provides opportunities for promotion, but it can be costly and slows down effective communication.

A hierarchical structure

A business with a **flat structure** has few levels of management but a wide span of control. This improves the business's flexibility but lines of authority are not always clear.

A flat structure

Organisation charts

A business's organisational structure can be shown using an organisation chart.

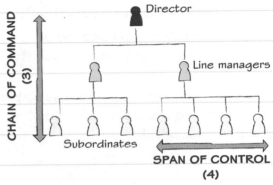

Line managers can pass on authority to their **subordinates** through **delegation**.

Centralised or decentralised?

- Centralised decisions are made by senior managers (normally at head office).
- Decentralised decisions are delegated to regional employees at local stores and branches.

Centralised	Decentralised
Increased control and standardisation	Decisions devolved to branches or divisions that may know their local customers better
Decisions can be slow	Loss of control

Size

As businesses expand they will naturally employ more people, increasing the **chain of command** and **span of control**. The size and structure of an organisation can have an impact on communication, control and flexibility of a business.

A business can **downsize** (reduce size) or **delayer** (reduce the number of layers in the hierarchy) to:

- reduce costs
- improve efficiency
- improve communication.

 Worked example

Explain **one** reason why a business might choose to reduce the number of layers in its organisational structure.   **(3 marks)**

Making an organisation's structure flatter can reduce costs and unnecessary employees. As a result, the organisation could operate more efficiently and this could lead to increased profitability.

You need to give a clear benefit of reducing the number of layers and then develop two arguments about the knock-on effect of this (such as operating more efficiently and increasing profitability).

Now try this

 1 Define the term 'span of control'.   **(1 mark)**

2 Explain **one** drawback to a business of having a long chain of command.   **(3 marks)**

The importance of effective communication

Good communication is extremely important in business. Effective communication ensures that the business's vision, mission and objectives are clear, that customers are able to understand its products and services, and that employees feel motivated because they understand their role within the business.

The communication process

For communication to be effective:

- the **sender** has to choose an appropriate **medium** to reach the **receiver**
- **feedback** should also be available to ensure the communication has been successful.

Impact of poor communication

Insufficient or excessive communication can have an impact on:

- ✓ employee motivation
- ✓ customer service
- ✓ the number of mistakes made
- ✓ the understanding of employees
- ✓ the efficient implementation of decisions
- ✓ the image/brand of the business (through advertising).

Types of communication

Formal communication is approved by the organisation. It follows set rules of communication used within a business.

Informal communication (e.g. gossip) is also used in business. It can get in the way of effective communication.

Barriers to effective communication

- Using inappropriate mediums or email system failure.
- Being angry or tired.
- Cultural differences.
- Use of jargon. This depends on the skill or knowledge of the sender or receiver.
- Too much or too little information.

Information overload

When workers are faced with too much information (e.g. receiving more than 100 emails a day or complicated instructions), their motivation and efficiency will fall. Managers must ensure communication is controlled and organised effectively to ensure that this does not happen.

Worked example

Explain **one** barrier to effective business communication.

(3 marks)

One barrier to effective communication is cultural differences. When a business is working with a foreign company, employees in the two businesses may not understand cultural references or meaning. This can lead to mistakes being made, such as the wrong product being shipped, which could lead to customers receiving the wrong products.

The student has developed their explanation with two points of development and given a relevant example.

Now try this

Discuss the likely benefit to a business of good communication.

(6 marks)

Different ways of working

People do not have to work for just one business operating from a particular location. The growth of technology and flexible working arrangements mean that employees can work from home or on the road, and businesses can employ workers when the need arises.

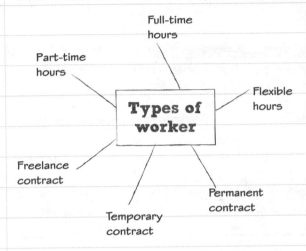

Full-time hours

Part-time hours

Types of worker

Flexible hours

Freelance contract

Temporary contract

Permanent contract

Flexible working

If a business can use flexible working contracts, it has more control over its costs and can increase or lower its capacity when it needs to. Freelance contracts are often used when a business needs to employ a specialist, such as a consultant or accountant, for a short period of time. However, the problem with flexible contracts is that employees might not be very committed to the business if they do not have long-term job security.

The impact of technology on ways of working

- **Remote working** – Employees can work from home while keeping in touch with colleagues through teleconferencing and email. Working arrangements can be agreed to meet the needs of the business and its workers, e.g. working from home one day a week.

- **Video conferencing** – Face-to-face communication and presentations can be streamed live over the internet so that employees no longer need to travel long distances to meet clients or share important information. This is more efficient as employees do not have to spend time and money travelling.

- **Management information systems** – Business intranet systems hold vast amounts of information that employees can access using a computer anywhere in the world.

Worked example

Discuss the impact on a business of employing workers on permanent contracts instead of flexible hours contracts. **(6 marks)**

With a permanent contract, employees will feel as though they have more job security and this may mean they are more motivated at work. As a result, they are going to be more productive. Furthermore, if an employee has a flexible hours contract, they may not have a guaranteed income and may look for a job elsewhere. This could lead to high rates of labour turnover, which may have an impact on the business's productivity and could result in a rise in recruitment costs.

The student has considered two reasons why one form of employment is better than another. They have also used business terms throughout and developed their answer.

Now try this

Define the term 'remote working'. **(1 mark)**

Different job roles and responsibilities

Within a business there is a wide range of roles, which all relate to one another to form the organisational structure. The role at the top of a business is the managing director (MD) or chief executive officer (CEO).

Key roles and responsibilities

Role	Responsible for...	Example
Directors	• overall business performance • business target-setting and strategy formation	A CEO setting profit targets and making key business decisions
Senior managers	• management and leadership of key business functions	The senior managers of a marketing department and the employees within it
Supervisors and team leaders	• leading a team of workers • performance management • providing training, support and motivation	A head waiter supervising a team of five waiting staff, monitoring performance and delivering on-the-job training
Operational staff	• carrying out the key operations of a business	A designer working in a fashion company
Support staff	• providing services that support the main function of a business	A secretary carrying out administrative work at a dentist's practice

The recruitment process

Draw up recruitment documents
Including job adverts, job particulars, job descriptions and job specifications

Receive applications
Through CVs, application forms and letters

Shortlisting
A list of suitable candidates is drawn up

Selection
Involves interviews and assessments; references might be requested

Training
To develop skills using on-the-job and off-the-job training (all staff, but especially new staff)

The candidate selected must have the right **skills** (e.g. the ability to operate computers or machines) and **attitudes** (e.g. flexibility or hardworking).

Shortlisting and selecting candidates

A number of documents are used in the recruitment process to help identify the best candidates. These include:

• application forms
• curriculum vitae (CV)
• job descriptions
• person specifications.

Worked example

Which **two** of the following documents are used in the recruitment process?
Select **two** answers: **(2 marks)**
☒ **A** Job description
☐ **B** Business plan
☐ **C** Person description
☒ **D** Application form
☐ **E** Cash-flow forecast

A person **specification** is used in recruitment, not a person **description**.

Now try this

Explain **one** reason why a business might employ team leaders.

(3 marks)

Effective recruitment

As small businesses grow, they may employ workers to fill new roles in the business. Businesses want the **right employees for the job**. The recruitment process is crucial in achieving this.

Job description

A job description contains the essential information about a job role. It will include:

- the job title
- who the person is responsible to (line manager)
- who the person is responsible for (subordinates)
- the key duties
- the salary or wage.

Person specification

A person specification contains a description of the characteristics, qualifications, experience and skills that are required to meet the needs of the job description. These factors are normally broken down into:

- essential characteristics (must have)
- desirable characteristics (would like).

Curriculum vitae (CV)

A CV is a document that lists a person's experience and qualifications, including details of their:

- education and qualifications
- employment history
- skills and experience
- references from current or previous employers.

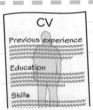

CV
Previous experience
Education
Skills

CVs can be used to give an employer an overview of the qualifications and experience of potential employees.

Types of recruitment

Internal recruitment	External recruitment
Promoting an employee who currently works for the business to a new role. 👍 Fast and easy to advertise vacancy. 👍 Cheaper than external advertising. 👍 Candidates already know the business so will be more efficient from the beginning. 👍 Promotion opportunities motivate current employees.	Recruiting someone who does not already work for the business. 👍 More potential applicants. 👍 New ideas and skills brought into the business. 👍 Suitable if the business is growing and needs more employees.

Techniques used to help identify the best candidate for a job may include interviews, tests, role plays, group discussions and candidate presentations.

Worked example

Explain **one** reason why a business might use external recruitment.　　(3 marks)

A business might use external recruitment if it intends to expand. By using external recruitment, the business will attract a wider number of new candidates from outside the organisation to help it grow in size. These candidates might also bring in new ideas and skills that help the business grow.

The student has shown a good understanding of external recruitment. The two points of development are linked to the reason that they have given (intending to expand).

Now try this

Define the term 'person specification'.　　(1 mark)

Developing employees

A business is only as good as its employees, which is why **employee development** is so important to businesses. Employee training and development improves the business's knowledge and skills.

Formal training

Employees attend specific training courses to improve their skills. These courses:

👍 may be provided by external companies who are subject or industry specialists

👍 may offer formal accreditation or qualifications

👎 can be expensive and time-consuming

👎 may require employees to stop working while they are training, so productivity falls.

Informal training

Employees learn skills 'on-the-job', by developing skills and experience over time or by being coached by other employees. This:

👍 is cheaper and less-time consuming than formal learning

👍 gives employees real or 'hands-on' experience

👎 may be stressful for employees if they are doing the job without all of the necessary skills

👎 may mean that employees have to take responsibility for seeking or providing training.

Performance management

All employees in a business should receive performance management. This involves setting targets for personal development and performance, and agreeing these targets with their line manager. Performance management may be used to support internal promotion and pay progression. Performance management meetings are formal and may take place several times a year.

It is likely that ongoing training will be made part of an employee's personal development, e.g. gaining relevant qualifications or attending external training courses. These may be set as targets.

Performance management form		
Outcomes	Deadline	Support
Target 1		
Target 2		
Target 3		

Performance management documents are a formal record of an agreement between an employee and their line manager.

Worked example

Explain **one** reason why a business might send its employees on an external training course. **(3 marks)**

A business might send its employees on an external course in order to develop new knowledge and skills. This means that the employees will then be better equipped to do their job and the productivity of the business will increase.

The student has developed their explanation, making a link between training employees and the impact that this will have on the business. Alternatively, the student could have explained that external training may bring skills into the business that do not already exist or may allow employees to be trained by recognised specialists in a particular subject or industry.

Now try this

Which **one** of the following is **not** a method of training employees?
Select **one** answer:

(1 mark)

☐ **A** Conferences

☐ **B** Observing colleagues work

☐ **C** Paying a good salary

☐ **D** Gaining a formal qualification

The importance of training

Skills – training employees will improve their skills and value to the business. Having the most skilled employees may give a business a competitive advantage over its rivals.

Motivation – as employees improve their skills and knowledge, their confidence will also improve. This can lead to a highly motivated and happy workforce.

> **The importance of training employees**

Retention – investing money in training employees shows that the business values its employees. This means they are less likely to leave to find a job elsewhere, so improving the business's retention rates.

Technology and training

New technology has benefits and drawbacks when training employees.

👍 New technology enables training as employees can use computer simulations (e.g. pilots and surgeons).

👍 Training can be more flexible and can be accessed remotely using webinars and online courses.

👎 Employees need to be retrained whenever new technology is introduced. This can be expensive and can lower productivity.

Self-learning

Employees can now take responsibility for their own learning. Many training courses are available online for employees to complete in their own time.

Technology can also be used to record employees' performances, e.g. a teacher can watch a video of one of their own lessons. This makes it easier for employees to monitor their performance and learn from experience.

Technology can be used as a low-risk method of training employees to do high-risk tasks.

Worked example

Define the term 'performance management'.   **(1 mark)**

Performance management is where employees are set targets for the year ahead. These targets may be linked to their pay and rewards.

Always try to make two clear points within a definition. For example, this student has mentioned 'targets' and 'pay and rewards', both of which are characteristics of performance management.

Now try this

Consider the trade-offs that a business faces when deciding whether to spend money on employee training. What else could they spend this money on?

Discuss the reasons why a business may choose not to invest in training its employees.   **(6 marks)**

Motivating employees 1

Motivation is an important factor in running a successful business. A highly motivated workforce is more committed to the business and will have a positive impact on customer relationships. Motivated employees are also more likely to continue working for the business and will be more productive.

A motivated workforce

Motivation can:

- ✓ create a hard-working and flexible workforce, that is willing to 'go the extra mile' for the business
- ✓ encourage employees to have greater commitment to the organisation
- ✓ reduce employee sick leave rates
- ✓ improve customer service
- ✓ improve communication within the business
- ✓ attract and retain good employees
- ✓ increase productivity because the workforce is happy.

Financial methods of motivation

Businesses often use a variety of financial methods, such as **remuneration**, to motivate their employees. Different methods work well for different types of role. For example, a commission-based structure works well for sales roles. Choosing the right remuneration method will maximise employees' productivity, whereas using the wrong method could waste money and fail to provide any benefit.

Time-based systems	Salaries	Results-based systems (suitable where output or success can be measured)	Fringe benefits	Career progression
• Wages for part-time or full-time workers • Overtime	• For non-manual jobs • For professional workers	• Piece rate • Commission • Bonus schemes	• Company car • Healthcare • Pension schemes • Company discounts	• Promotion

Worked example

Give **two** other financial methods of motivation, apart from salary and payment by the hour, that a business could use to reward employees.

(2 marks)

1   Piece rate
2   Commission

There is no need to explain in a 'give' question.

How important is money?

Most people think that receiving a fair income is important. However, some theories of motivation state that money alone is not enough to fully motivate people in the workplace. Other needs are as important or even more important motivating factors, such as self-esteem and the freedom to be creative.

Good personal relationships at work can be an important motivating factor.

Now try this

Explain **one** benefit to a business of rewarding workers using a piece rate system.   **(3 marks)**

Motivating employees 2

Job rotation – gives employees the opportunity to work in other areas of the business, experience different roles and develop new skills.

Job enrichment – develops employees' skills by giving them opportunities to lead, make key decisions and take on new responsibilities.

Non-financial methods of motivation

Teamworking – allows employees to develop social bonds through being part of a team.

Employee reward scheme – recognises employees' performance and contribution through schemes, e.g. employee of the week.

Empowering employees

NEWS

20% time

Google used to have a policy known as '20% time'. This gave employees the freedom to devote one day every week to a creative project of their choice, in order to develop new innovative products and solutions to problems. Many businesses have adopted similar policies, with the intention of motivating employees by giving them more creative freedom in their roles.

Autonomy

Autonomy means being empowered to make your own decisions. Employees are often more motivated when they can make their own decisions and choices about the best way to work and achieve their goals.

Worked example

Discuss the likely benefit to a business of rewarding the achievements of its employees. **(6 marks)**

By rewarding the achievements of its employees, a business will be helping to motivate its workforce. This is because the employees will feel pride and gain greater self-esteem as a result of their achievements at work being recognised. As a result, employees will feel valued and work harder. This can lead to higher levels of productivity and better customer service. Motivated workers are also less likely to leave the business, which means lower recruitment and training costs. These savings can be put into the financial rewards, such as bonuses, for employees to further boost motivation.

The student has developed their answer with several benefits of having a motivated workforce.

Now try this

Explain **one** advantage to a business of adopting job rotation. **(3 marks)**

Case study

In Sections B and C of Paper 2, you will have to review a full-page case study before answering questions. You should aim to spend about 10 minutes reading the case study before you attempt to answer any questions. Have a look at the sample case study below, then look at the worked examples on the next five pages.

Deliveroo

Deliveroo is a takeaway food delivery service that was established in 2013. The business's smartphone app and website allows customers to browse and order from restaurants in their local area, with Deliveroo charging diners a £2.50 fee for the service. Deliveroo uses a network of self-employed cyclists to deliver takeaway food from these restaurants.

Between 2013 and 2017, the business raised more than $400 million from investors and was considered to be one of the UK's most promising technology companies. Deliveroo employs more than 3000 delivery staff in the UK and said in 2017 that its delivery staff can earn an average of £12 per hour, depending on their location. However, its employees do not receive the benefits associated with being a full-time employee as they are considered contract workers.

Deliveroo operates in a growing but competitive market. In 2016, the business achieved revenues of £130 million from operations in more than 10 countries worldwide. In the summer of 2017, it moved into a new London office and plans to create 300 new jobs.

However, Deliveroo is facing increased competition, such as from the taxi app business Uber, which launched a London-based food delivery service called UberEATS in 2016.

Figure 1: Value of worldwide takeaway delivery brands (2016)

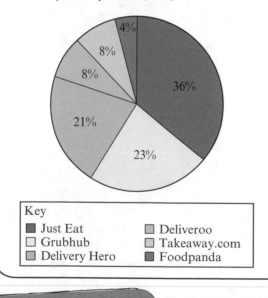

Key
- ■ Just Eat
- □ Grubhub
- ▨ Delivery Hero
- ▨ Deliveroo
- □ Takeaway.com
- ■ Foodpanda

Figure 2: Percentage of takeaways ordered online and delivered in the UK

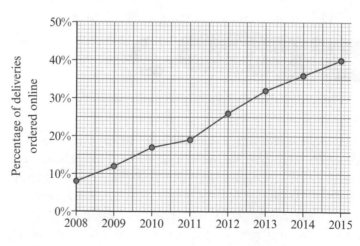

Source: The NPD Group/CREST®, year ending June 2015

Now try this

Read the case study above.

(a) Highlight all of the key business terminology in the case study.

(b) Identify **one** human resource decision that Deliveroo has made.

(c) List the benefits and the drawbacks of Deliveroo's business model.

Short-answer questions

Worked example

Define the term 'self-employed'. **(1 mark)**

Self-employed refers to someone who works for themselves and does not have a permanent contract to work for a business.

This is a good answer. The student could also have made reference to self-employed people not having the same benefits and rights as full-time employed workers.

'Define' questions

Try to answer a 'define' question in no more than two sentences.

Links Look at the glossary on page 93 for definitions of key business terminology.

Quantitative skills **'Identify' questions**

An 'identify' question requires you to interpret information from a source, such as charts, graphs, infographics, text or financial accounts.

Quantitative skills The student has interpreted the pie chart correctly to identify Just Eat as the business with the largest value. This would suggest they are the market leader.

Worked example

Using the information in Figure 1 (see page 86), identify the worldwide market leader in the takeaway delivery industry in 2016.

(1 mark)

Just Eat

Links You can revise interpreting graphs and charts on page 75.

Worked example

Outline **one** method of raising capital that could be used by a limited company such as Deliveroo. **(2 marks)**

A limited company such as Deliveroo could raise capital through selling shares in the company. However, it could not raise capital by selling shares to the public as it is not a public limited company.

'Outline' questions

An 'outline' question should always give a point with some form of development or explanation. The answer must also be in context.

The student's answer is in context since the method identified is appropriate for a private limited company. There is also some development in relation to the limitations of share capital as a private limited company.

Links You can revise raising capital to finance growth on page 51.

Now try this

Outline **one** reason why Deliveroo might use self-employed cyclists and drivers. **(2 marks)**

'Calculate' questions

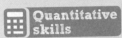 **Using the case study**

In this 'calculate' question, the student has been given one piece of information (net profit £15 million). The student also has to use the case study to identify the other piece of information needed to complete the net profit margin calculation (sales revenue of £130 million).

 This student has learned the net profit margin formula and their answer shows their workings so it is clear to see how they have reached the answer.

Links You can revise net profit margin on page 74.

Worked example

Consider a scenario whereby Deliveroo generated a net profit of £15 million in 2016. Taking the above statement to be true, calculate the net profit margin for Deliveroo in 2016. You are advised to show your workings. **(2 marks)**

LEARN IT!

Net profit margin = $\dfrac{\text{Net profit}}{\text{Sales revenue}} \times 100$

$\dfrac{£15\ \text{million}}{£130\ \text{million}} = 0.11538$

$0.11538 \times 100 = 11.54\%$

2016 net profit margin = 11.54%

Worked example

Using the information in Figure 2 (see page 86), calculate the percentage growth rate of the UK online order and delivery market since Deliveroo launched in 2013. You are advised to show your workings. **(2 marks)**

LEARN IT!

% growth = $\dfrac{\text{Increase in size}}{\text{Original size}} \times 100$

$\dfrac{8}{32} = 0.25$

$0.25 \times 100 = 25\%$

Market growth = 25%

 The student has used Figure 2 to work out that there has been an increase of 8 percentage points (32% to 40%) since Deliveroo launched in 2013.

 Calculating percentage increase

Percentage increase is a key calculation that you may have to perform in your exam. This could be a percentage increase in sales revenue, profit, costs, interest rates or market growth.

A common mistake might have been to give 8% as the answer. However, this is simply the increase in the proportion of takeaway meals that are ordered online for delivery, not the growth of the online order and delivery market.

Now try this

Natalya is planning to set up her own takeaway delivery business. The following information is taken from her business plan.

Year 1 sales revenue: £20 000

Year 1 cost of sales: £13 725

Calculate Natalya's expected gross profit margin in Year 1. **(2 marks)**

'Analyse' questions

Worked example

Analyse the impact on Deliveroo of not having its own restaurants. **(6 marks)**

As Deliveroo does not have its own restaurant businesses, it is able to keep its overhead costs very low. Even though Deliveroo has a head office in London, it does not need to rent expensive locations or have bases from which its delivery drivers work. With low overheads, Deliveroo is able to make a greater contribution towards profits on every order that it delivers.

One issue with not having its own restaurants is that Deliveroo relies on partnerships with restaurant businesses. If Deliveroo's suppliers (the restaurants) decided not to use the business or agreed contracts with other firms such as Just Eat, then Deliveroo could quickly go out of business. If Deliveroo eventually grew into its own restaurant chain, then it would start to gain economies of scale as it would be able to make a greater profit on every order it delivers.

How else could you link this answer to the context of Deliveroo? Try to identify two issues relating to Deliveroo that you might connect in your own answer to this question.

'Analyse' questions

An 'analyse' question is very similar to the 'discuss' questions that you will find in Section A of Paper 1 and Paper 2. However, an 'analyse' question needs to be answered in the context of the case study. For example, an answer in context may use specific information in the case study to make assumptions or conclusions. It may also apply the nature of the business (Deliveroo is a delivery business) or the nature of the product (takeaway food).

The first paragraph in this answer explains a benefit to Deliveroo of not running its own restaurants (low overhead costs). Another benefit might be that Deliveroo can focus on its core business of delivery, rather than having to compete in the takeaway food market.

This answer is clearly in context because the student refers to Deliveroo's 'head office' and competitors such as 'Just Eat'.

The second paragraph analyses the limitations of Deliveroo not having its own restaurants. The student has explored the relationship between Deliveroo and its suppliers. The student could have also discussed the fact that Deliveroo can only make a small profit on each delivery. As the business grows, it could expand into other markets in order to increase its potential profits.

Your answer needs to consider the context of the case study (in this case, Deliveroo).

Now try this

Analyse the impact on Deliveroo of using self-employed workers instead of permanent employees. **(6 marks)**

'Justify' questions

'Justify' questions

A 'justify' question requires you to consider two different options. This might include considering the relative benefits and drawbacks of two alternative strategies. Your answer will need to be in context and must finish with a justified conclusion based on your analysis.

Balance

A balanced answer identifies the benefits and drawbacks of something. Using balance is a good technique when answering 'justify' and 'evaluate' questions.

The student has shown an understanding of customer needs and considered the advantages and disadvantages of Option 1.

The student has shown an understanding of the benefits and drawbacks of advertising. They have also demonstrated context by giving an example of a competitor ('Hungry House') and referring specifically to the Deliveroo app ('download the app').

🔗 **Links** You can revise advertising on pages 63 and 64.

This paragraph gives the student's conclusion. They have made a decision and provided a justification for their choice, as well as explaining a limitation of the option they have not chosen.

Worked example

Deliveroo is looking to expand its business and is considering one of two options to increase sales. The two options are:
Option 1: Increasing the number of restaurants it works with
Option 2: Promoting the Deliveroo app through advertising
Justify which **one** of these two options would most help Deliveroo increase sales. **(9 marks)**

Increasing the number of partner restaurants could allow Deliveroo to offer a wider range of products to its customers, such as different types of food or food from less common cuisines. This could attract more customers as there may be people whose needs are not being met by the current range of foods delivered by Deliveroo. It may also help it to expand into new areas of the UK, where customer needs may not be fulfilled. However, increasing the range of restaurants may take a long time so will not increase sales in the short term.

On the other hand, promoting the Deliveroo app will make people more aware of the service that Deliveroo offers. This will encourage people to download the app and try the service, especially if Deliveroo introduces a special offer such as free delivery on the first order. Furthermore, promoting the app might encourage some customers who already use other delivery services, such as Hungry House, to switch to Deliveroo. On the other hand, increasing advertising will increase the business's costs.

Overall, I believe it is better for Deliveroo to spend money advertising its app. Although building links with more restaurants will increase customers' choice, it will not directly increase the number of people using Deliveroo in the short term as it already delivers for a wide range of restaurants. The decision may depend on the popularity of the restaurants that Deliveroo is in partnership with.

The student has made good use of an 'it depends' statement.

Now try this

Deliveroo is considering two different options to finance its plans to expand into a new country. The two options are as follows.

Option 1: Raising additional share capital from investors
Option 2: Crowd funding

Justify which **one** of these two options would be the most appropriate method of financing its plans. **(9 marks)**

'Evaluate' questions

Evaluate the impact on Deliveroo's long-term success of not providing its delivery workers the same rights as permanent employees. You should use the information provided as well as your knowledge of business.   **(12 marks)**

Improving an answer

By paying its delivery staff as contract workers, Deliveroo has been able to create a flexible workforce and to employ people who are looking for both full- and part-time work delivering for the company. By having a flexible workforce, Deliveroo can keep costs down which has meant that the capital it has raised could be invested in developing the app, building relationships with restaurants and promoting the brand. Furthermore, this approach has kept labour costs low and, although we do not know how much profit Deliveroo made in its first three years, this will certainly have helped the business achieve a good profit margin. Using contract workers also makes it easier to recruit the 3000 delivery workers that Deliveroo needs in order to meet demand.

...Overall, paying delivery staff as contractors has allowed Deliveroo to be very competitive because it does not have to pay National Insurance and offer holiday or sick pay. This has led to Deliveroo being able to grow very quickly in its first three years of trading. However, to secure the long-term success of the business, it is important that Deliveroo starts to invest in its workers now that it can afford to do so, in order to ensure that its ethical reputation is not damaged, which may cause customers to choose other delivery services that provide better conditions for their employees.

The student's first paragraph offers a number of limitations and drawbacks for Deliveroo of not providing its workers with employment benefits.

This is just part of a student answer. It is **not** a model answer. It is a sample answer for you to improve.

The second paragraph of this answer has not been included here. However, this paragraph might look at some of the limitations or risks of not providing its delivery workers with benefits and good working conditions.

The student has used their knowledge of ethics and motivation to answer this question.

 Links Turn to page 57 for a reminder about ethics. Turn to pages 84 and 85 to revise motivation.

Marking an 'evaluate' answer

The following bullet points are taken from Level 3 (9–12 marks) of the mark scheme used to mark an 'evaluate' question. Do you think the student's answer meets these criteria?

☑ Demonstrates accurate knowledge and understanding of business concepts and issues throughout, including appropriate use of business terminology (AO1b).

☑ Detailed application of knowledge and understanding of business concepts and issues to the business context throughout (AO2).

☑ Deconstructs business information and/ or issues, finding detailed interconnected points with logical chains of reasoning (AO3a).

☑ Draws a valid and well-reasoned conclusion based on a thorough evaluation of business information and issues (AO3b).

Now try this

Ensure that the paragraph you write is in the context of Deliveroo.

Write the second paragraph needed to complete the student's answer to the 'evaluate' question.

Formulae

You will not be given these formulae in the exam, so you need to learn them!

LEARN IT!

Total costs

Total costs (TC) = Total fixed costs (TFC) + Total variable costs (TVC)

Variable costs

Variable costs = Cost of one unit × Quantity produced

Revenue

Revenue = Price × Quantity

Break-even

$$\text{Break-even point in units} = \frac{\text{Fixed costs}}{\text{(Sales price − Variable cost)}}$$

Break-even point in costs / Revenue = Break-even point in units × Sales price

Margin of safety

Margin of safety = Actual or budgeted sales − Break-even sales

Interest (on loans)

$$\text{Interest (on loans) in \%} = \frac{\text{Total repayment − Borrowed amount}}{\text{Borrowed amount}} \times 100$$

Net cash flow

Net cash flow = Cash inflows (receipts) − Cash outflows in a given period (payments)

Opening and closing balances

Opening balance = Closing balance of the previous period

Closing balance = Opening balance + Net cash flow

Profit

Profit / loss = Total revenue − Total costs

Gross profit

Gross profit = Sales revenue − Cost of sales

Gross profit margin

$$\text{Gross profit margin (\%)} = \frac{\text{Gross profit}}{\text{Sales revenue}} \times 100$$

Net profit

Net profit = Gross profit − Other operating expenses and interest

Net profit margin

$$\text{Net profit margin (\%)} = \frac{\text{Net profit}}{\text{Sales revenue}} \times 100$$

Average rate of return

$$\text{Average rate of return (\%)} = \frac{\text{Average annual profit (Total profit / No. of years)}}{\text{Cost of investment}} \times 100$$

Percentage growth

$$\text{Percentage growth} = \frac{\text{Increase in size}}{\text{Original size}} \times 100$$

Glossary

Asset: any item of value that a business owns, such as its machinery or premises.

Bank overdraft: a facility offered by a bank that allows an account holder to borrow money at short notice.

Biased: unbalanced or inclined to agree with a particular judgement or idea rather than presenting the evidence fairly.

Brand loyalty: a customer's willingness to buy a product from a particular business rather than from its competitors.

Business plan: a document that outlines how an entrepreneur is going to set up a new business.

Competitive advantage: an advantage a business has over its rivals that is unique and sustainable.

Consumer: someone who buys and uses goods and services.

Convenience: a product or service's ability to fit in well with a customer's lifestyle or routine, the ease with which it can be used and/or its easy-to-reach location.

Customer base: the clients who buy the products/services of a business, a proportion of whom are repeat customers.

Demographics: relating to the structure of a population.

Differentiate: show that a product is different from similar products.

E-commerce: using the internet to carry out business transactions.

Enterprise: a person or organisation with the purpose of producing goods and services to meet the needs of customers (can also mean entrepreneurial activity).

Entrepreneur: someone who creates a business, taking on financial risks with the aim of making a profit from the business.

E-tailing: retailing to customers through the internet, such as through an e-commerce website.

Exports: the flow of goods and services out of a country and into another country.

Imports: the flow of goods and services into a country from another country.

Innovation: changing an existing product or process.

Interest: the cost of borrowing, or a percentage of the amount of money borrowed that must be repaid in addition to the original amount borrowed.

Invention: creating something completely new.

Investment: putting money into a business with the intention of making a profit.

Legislation: the laws that a business must comply with.

Logistics: the organisation and management of the transport of raw materials and goods.

Marketing mix: the 4 Ps of marketing, which are product, price, promotion and place.

Market research: the process of gathering information about the market and customers' needs and wants in order to help inform business decisions, including product design and marketing.

Market share: the proportion of sales in a market that are taken by one business.

Motivated: when an employee has reasons for working well and increasing their productivity.

Multinational: a business with operations in more than one country (also known as a multinational corporation or MNC).

Obsolete: out of date or no longer used.

Partnership: a business that is owned by a group of two or more people who share the financial risk, the decision-making and the profits.

Pressure group: a group of people who join together to try to influence government policy or business policy for a particular cause.

Price point: the point on a scale of possible prices at which a business fixes the price of its product.

Private limited company: an incorporated business that is owned by shareholders who invest in the business in return for a share of the profits and voting rights at the annual general meeting (AGM).

Profit: the amount of revenue left over once costs have been deducted.

Profit margin: the proportion of revenue left over after costs have been deducted.

Public limited company: an incorporated business that can sell shares to the public (also known as a PLC).

Qualitative: concerning the quality of something that cannot be measured in numbers.

Quantitative: concerning the quantity or amount of something that can be measured in numbers.

Reasonable care: taking enough care to ensure that a product or service is suitable for customers, such as providing a meal that can be eaten.

Redundancy procedures: the process through which a business stops employing some of its staff because their roles are no longer needed.

Reliable: (of data) representative of a wider group or the population as a whole.

Repeat purchases: products or services that are repeatedly purchased by the same group of customers (these can be seen as a measure of customer loyalty).

Retailing: selling products or services to customers in a physical shop.

Retained profit: money that a business keeps, rather than paying out to its shareholders.

Revenue: the money that comes into a business from sales.

Reward: the money that an entrepreneur or investor receives when a business succeeds.

Risk: the possibility that an enterprise will have lower than anticipated profits or experience a loss.

Roles: the different jobs within a business.

Share capital: money that is raised by a business issuing shares that it then sells to those who wish to invest in the company.

Shareholders: investors who are part-owners of a company.

Social media: websites that allow users to interact with other users, by sharing text-based messages, pictures or links to online content.

Sole trader: a type of unincorporated business that is owned by just one person.

Span of control: the number of employees that are managed by a manager (e.g. if a person manages three employees, their span of control is three).

Start-up: a new business, usually with only a small number of employees – perhaps only one.

Stock: the products held by a business in a shop or warehouse, usually for sale to customers.

Stock exchange: a place where shares in PLCs can be bought and sold.

Trade credit: a credit arrangement that is offered only to businesses by suppliers.

Unique selling point (USP): something that makes a product or service stand out from its competitors.

Venture capital: money that a business sources from individuals, or groups of people, who wish to invest their own money into new businesses.

Answers

Theme 1: Investigating small business

The following pages contain suggested answers to the 'Now try this' questions in Theme 1 of the Revision Guide. In many cases, these are not the only correct answers.

1. The dynamic nature of business

1 The introduction of new technology will create the opportunity to develop new products. New technology can also help to improve the current features of many products. This means that a business could add new features and benefits that will make its products more desirable to customers.

2 A gap in the market can give rise to new opportunities because it means there is little/no competition in the market. This means that a business that positions itself in this gap is likely to attract the customers who fill that segment of the market, but will have no competition to contend with.

2. Risk and reward

Setting up their own business means that they will get to make all of their own decisions and run the business how they want. This will increase their personal satisfaction.

3. The role of business enterprise

A business may find it difficult to add value to its products or services if the product/service it sells is very generic. This means that many other businesses might sell the same product and there is very little difference between them (e.g. milk). This means that the business may find it difficult to differentiate its products from the competition and the only way it will be able to compete is by lowering the price. In turn, this could have a significant impact on its profit margins. If a business cannot add value to its product/service, there is very little reason for a customer to buy from it, unless its prices are competitive.

4. The importance of added value

D

5. The role of entrepreneurship

A and C

6. Customer needs 1

If a business provides high-quality products, it will be meeting customer needs because its products will be durable. This means that they will last a long time without the customer needing to replace them.

7. Customer needs 2

B

8. The role of market research

A business may conduct market research before it starts trading in order to understand the needs of its customers. If a business understands its customer needs, it will be better equipped to provide products and services that meet these needs. A business may also carry out research to understand its competitors. If a business understands its competitors and what they offer, it will be able to make plans to differentiate its products or to provide products and services that offer better value for money than its rivals.

9. Types of market research

A

10. Market research data

1 Market research is the process of gathering information about customers, competitors and market trends through primary or secondary sources.

2 Suggested answers could include: questionnaires, surveys, tally count, observations, answers with a scale response.

3 Market research data will enable a business to find out how many people are interested in its product or might be willing to buy it. As a result, the business can decide whether the product is appropriate for customers and if enough people will buy it to make a profit.

11. Market segmentation

1 A market segment is a specific group of customers who have similar characteristics and needs.

2 A business may choose to segment its market in order to target a specific group of customers. By doing this it will be better equipped to meet customer needs and this may result in a greater level of sales as more customers will be attracted to buy its products.

12. Market mapping

B and D

13. Competition

C and E

14. Competitive markets

1 Suggested answers could include:
- quality
- unique name
- packaging
- customer service.

2 A differentiated product might help a business to stand out in the market. This means that customers are more likely to notice the product and this could lead to increased sales.

15. Aims and objectives

B

16. Differing aims and objectives

1 Suggested answers could include:
- independence and control
- challenge
- social benefits or goals
- customer satisfaction
- business awards and recognition
- personal satisfaction.

2 Market share refers to the percentage of the whole market that a business controls. This can be a percentage of products sold or a percentage of total sales value.

17. Revenues and costs

(i)   £7000
(ii) £5000
(iii) £5000
(iv) £7000

18. Profit and loss

C

19. Break-even charts

£800 000

20. Using break-even

1 The break-even point will rise.
2 One limitation of using a break-even chart is that it is very difficult to construct a break-even chart if a business sells multiple product lines. This means that it is harder to produce an accurate break-even chart. As a result, the decisions made using the break-even chart will be flawed.

21. Calculating cash-flow

B

22. The importance of cash to a business

A business could improve its cash flow by ensuring that its customers all pay on time. This would more quickly increase the flow of money into the business and would mean that the business would have the cash available to pay for its expenses. This is especially important if a business has to pay for its expenses, such as stock, up-front.

23. Short-term sources of finance

A business might use a bank overdraft to pay for short-term costs such as supplier bills. This will ensure that it does not get behind with any payments and damage the relationship it has with its suppliers.

24. Long-term sources of finance

A and E

25. Limited liability

D

26. Types of business ownership

1 Suggested answers could include:
   • accounts have to be made public
   • more information must be reported to the government
   • more complex to set up than a sole trader or partnership
   • shareholders may disagree.
2 Limited liability is when the owners of the business are not liable for the debts of the business and can only lose the amount of capital that they have invested.

27. Franchising

One drawback of running a franchise is that the franchisee has to pay a royalty payment to the franchisor. This means that a percentage of sales revenue is lost and this can reduce the profit margins of the business.

28. Business location

Locating a business on the outskirts of a large city may be cheaper than if it were located in a city centre. This is because land value (rent and mortgage costs) are far higher in busy cities. This means that locating on the outskirts would help reduce fixed costs for the business. The savings made through having lower fixed costs would reduce break-even and help the business to achieve profits sooner, providing customers are still aware of and willing to travel to the business.

29. The marketing mix

1 A business might charge a higher price for a product or service if its market research indicated that customers were willing to pay a higher price. This would allow the business to achieve a greater profit margin per unit sold and increase its overall profits.
2 A business might choose to use social media such as Twitter to promote its products because so many people now use social media networks. As a result, a wider range of people will see the posts and this will lead to greater brand awareness for the business.

30. Influences on the marketing mix

C and E

31. The business plan

B and E

32. The nature of business planning

A business would include financial forecasts in a business plan because any potential lender will want to see this information. If a lender can see financial forecasts that show the business is likely to have a positive cash flow and eventually to make a profit, then they will be more willing to lend it money.

33. Stakeholders

D

34. Stakeholder conflict

1 A stakeholder is a group with an interest in the activities or performance of a business.
2 In this case, the local community is the stakeholder with the most influence. This is because the local community was concerned about the impact of Gerrard PLC's new plant and protested against the proposal, resulting in the business changing its plans.

35. Technology and business

The benefit of using digital communications such as email with customers is that it allows the business to keep customers up to date with special offers and new product launches. Emails can be sent out automatically to customers who have signed up and given their permission. This can help the business build relationships with its customers and ensure they are aware of what the business is doing without the business having to pay for expensive advertising. Digital communications will also improve the standards of customer service. If customers are updated on their orders, they will feel more assured. This will mean they have a better experience dealing with the business and are more likely to return in the future.

36. Principles of consumer law

One disadvantage for a business of new consumer protection law is that it may influence how the business produces its products, e.g. requiring extra safety features. This means that the business must add extra features and this is likely to increase its variable costs. This, in turn, will lower its profit margins.

37. Principles of employment law

One disadvantage for a business of new employment protection law is that it could increase its recruitment or training costs by requiring that staff have additional skills or knowledge in order to do their jobs, e.g. health and safety training. This is likely to lower profit margins as fixed costs will increase. As a result, the business may decide to employ fewer people.

38. The economy and business

If consumer confidence falls, this could mean that they are worried about the future. This means they will be more likely to save their money, as opposed to spending it. This will result in a fall in demand for most products.

39. Unemployment and inflation

High levels of unemployment might mean that a business finds it easier to recruit employees. This is because there are likely to be more applicants who come forward for any potential post. As a result, the business will have more people to choose from and is more likely to find the right person for both the role and the business.

40. Interest rates

If interest rates rise, this may increase the business's costs if it has taken out a loan from a bank. As a result, its cash-flow position may worsen as it covers the additional costs of repaying the loan. This could result in the business struggling to operate and pay its other costs.

41. Exchange rates

B

42. External influences

A business may respond to a fall in economic activity by cutting back on employees. As demand will be lower, a business will not need as many employees. Also, making some employees redundant may be a way of reducing costs and saving money. However, this approach could have a negative impact on employee morale and therefore on productivity. Another option might be for the business to lower its prices. Lower prices may encourage customers to keep buying its products, enabling the business to maintain sales and keep its employees in work. If the business can do this successfully, it could even act as a competitive advantage over rival businesses.

43. Exam skills: Case study

(a) Social media, break-even, costs, revenues, average price, variable cost, total revenue, total costs, fixed costs.

(b) Answers might include:
- caters for outdoor events
- uses the finest ingredients
- customers are able to design their own creations.

(c) Benefits might include:
- high levels of customer satisfaction
- relatively low fixed costs
- flexibility – able to cater for a wide variety of events.

Drawbacks might include:
- seasonality of outdoor events
- cost of importing ingredients from abroad
- could the business model be easy for someone else to copy?

44. Exam skills: Short-answer questions 1

Providing a flexible service, such as producing personalised pizzas with unusual toppings, allows The Wood Fired Pizza Company to meet customer needs. This will increase its customers' brand loyalty.

45. Exam skills: Short-answer questions 2

The Wood Fired Pizza Company could improve its cash flow by negotiating with suppliers of pizza bases, cheeses and other pizza ingredients to accept payment later.

46. Exam skills: 'Analyse' questions

Suggested links or issues could include:
- having limited liability may make it easier for Joe to attract investors and raise finance (e.g. to expand the business) because investors are likely to consider an incorporated business less risky
- a trade-off of having limited liability could be that the business's financial information is no longer kept private (if the business becomes a private limited company).

47. Exam skills: 'Justify' questions

Importing ingredients from Italy could benefit the business by improving the quality of its products and enabling the business to exploit this improved quality as a competitive advantage. Similarly, imported Italian ingredients could also improve the product's authenticity. For example, the reviewer quoted in the case study mentions the fact that the pizzas 'remind us of Italy', and using ingredients imported from Italy could allow The Wood Fired Pizza Company to emphasise this in its advertising. This emphasis on authenticity could give it a competitive advantage over similar businesses in the market and allow it to charge a premium price for its more authentically Italian pizzas. However, importing ingredients could also increase the business's costs. This means that Joe would need to decide whether importing ingredients would increase revenue enough to cover the increased costs.

48. Exam skills: 'Evaluate' questions

Overall, having well-trained employees with the right food hygiene qualifications will have a limited impact on the success of the business. This is because, while it may be a legal requirement of running a food preparation business without which The Wood Fired Pizza Company could not trade, customers expect to receive safe and hygienically prepared food, so this training cannot be exploited as a competitive advantage. Of course, this depends on the level of the training or on the quality of training undertaken by competitor's staff. Training all of their staff to a level well above the minimum standard, as in this case, may offer The Wood Fired Pizza Company a competitive advantage.

Theme 2: Building a business

The following pages contain suggested answers to the 'Now try this' questions in Theme 2 of the Revision Guide. In many cases, these are not the only correct answers.

49. Business growth

A

50. Public limited companies (PLCs)

One disadvantage of becoming a PLC is that the directors cannot control who buys the company's shares once they have been issued on a stock market. This means that the business is open to takeover, which could limit the control the directors have over the business.

51. Financing growth

1 Suggested answers could include:
- loan capital
- sale of assets
- retained profit
- owner's funds.

2 One benefit of loan capital is that it can potentially be for a substantial amount of capital if the bank agrees that the investment is safe and the business can repay the loan. This means that the loan capital could finance a new business investment and provide financial security for the first year of trading.

52. Why business objectives change

C

53. How business objectives change

A business might set an objective to increase recruitment if it believes that there are opportunities for expansion. Recruitment will bring in new employees with new ideas and this could lead to increased productivity.

54. Business and globalisation

1 Globalisation is the process of the world becoming ever more interconnected through communication, trade and culture.

2 One disadvantage of globalisation for a UK company is that its market is open to foreign competition. This means that the business may have more businesses to compete with and this could lead to them owning a smaller percentage of the market.

55. International trade

1 Suggested answers could include:
- protect jobs in domestic industries
- protect infant industries
- prevent the dumping of cheap goods on the domestic market
- raise revenue from tariffs
- prevent the entry of undesirable goods.

2 One drawback of a quota on imports is that it can restrict the quantity of a product that is brought into a country. This may mean that a business cannot buy enough resources to make its products. This could result in the business having to purchase more expensive resources from other sources.

56. Competing internationally

Changing its product to meet the needs of customers in a different country, who may have different tastes, will allow a business to increase its customers' brand loyalty and, therefore, increase its market share in that country.

57. Ethics and business

1 Suggested answers could include:
- lobbying
- protests.

2 One disadvantage for a business of being ethical is that making ethical decisions can increase costs in the short term. This could mean that the business finds it harder to make a profit and some investors may not be happy if they do not see their investment making a short-term return.

58. Environmental issues

Suggested answers could include:
- noise pollution
- air pollution
- traffic congestion
- resource depletion.

59. Product 1

Balancing a product's design mix can help a business to attract new customers and encourage brand loyalty, giving it a competitive advantage over rival businesses. This is because a balanced design mix can produce a product that is appealing to customers, does its job and is sold at a price that customers are willing to pay.

60. Product 2

Suggested answers may include:
- improve the quality of the product
- improve customer service.

61. The importance of price

1 Suggested answers might include:
- price is linked to revenue
- price is linked to profit
- price should represent the value of the product or service.

2 A business might set a premium price for its products in order to maximise its profits.

62. Pricing strategies

A business may only have to sell low volumes of its products to be profitable if it makes a high margin on each item. One way that it might be able to do this is if the product is bespoke, unique and rare. Customers are often willing to pay a premium price for something that has a unique selling point, such as a one-off painting or piece of architecture. When a business can add lots of value in this way and manage its costs, then it may be able to sell products with a very high profit margin, meaning that it need only sell small quantities to make a profit.

63. Promotion

Product trials allow customers to try a product for free, which means that a business can distribute free samples of a product without having to convince customers to buy it, thereby increasing the amount of exposure that the product gets. Customers that like the free trial are then more likely to buy the product than if they had not sampled it first.

64. Promotion, branding and technology

1 Viral advertising is when a business's promotional message, video or image is distributed and shared among a lot of people on social networks.

2 A business may choose to launch its own app because this allows its customers to engage with the business easily. This means that it is easier for a business to communicate with its customers by sharing details of new products and offers. As a result, customers are more likely to buy its products.

65. Place

D

66. Integrated marketing mix

The marketing mix can help a business gain a competitive advantage because the development of the 4 Ps helps a business to create a unique proposition for its customers. By focusing on its products, a business can differentiate them against rival businesses' products so that they are more desirable. A prime business location represents place in the marketing mix, and this could help a business attract more customers than its rivals. Also, it is an advantage that is very difficult for another business to copy. Ultimately, a well-integrated marketing mix where each element of the 4 Ps works effectively with the others will help a business provide the right product, at the right price and at the right time. This can lead to a competitive advantage if it is done better than a rival company.

67. Business operations and production

Job production is where a business makes unique or bespoke products that are a one-off. This can require employing a skilled workforce.

68. Business operations and technology

Suggested answers could include:
- reduce number of workers
- use more automation
- switch suppliers for cheaper resources
- reduce waste.

69. Managing stock

25 units

70. Suppliers and procurement

1 Stock refers to the materials a business uses to make its products. It can also represent finished goods ready for sale.

2 One factor a business may consider when choosing a supplier is how flexible they are. A flexible supplier might be important if the business has to adapt to customer needs quickly. By using a flexible supplier, a business might avoid missing opportunities to sell to customers who need a rapid response or quick sale.

71. Managing quality

Achieving a high standard of quality will improve customer satisfaction. This could lead to repeat purchases and therefore increased sales revenue.

72. Customer service and the sales process

Suggested answers could include:
- reputation for poor customer service
- loss of custom
- complaints and negative publicity
- low levels of repeat purchase.

73. Gross and net profit

A business will calculate its gross profit to understand the profit it has made on its trading activity. This will help it to understand how effectively it is selling its products or services and will allow it to make decisions on costs and prices.

74. Profit margins and ARR

The average rate of return is the average annual amount of profit generated over the life of an investment.

75. Interpreting quantitative business data

A business might use historical sales revenue figures to predict its future sales. Past data may give the business an indication of how much it could sell in the future. A business can then make sure that it has enough stock to meet this demand.

76. Limitations of quantitative data

A business should be cautious when using financial data to make business decisions because financial data only informs a business of financial performance. It does not give the business an insight into the attitudes of its customers or their reasons for purchasing the product or service. For example, poor financial performance may be explained by a slow-down in the economy and have little to do with poor business performance. Another reason is that financial data is always historical. This means that it is a representation of what happened in the past and this can often be a poor indicator of what will happen in the future or the current position of the business. A business should always use financial data alongside other information on the market and other indicators of the business's performance.

77. Organisational structures

1 The span of control represents the number of subordinates a line manager is responsible for in a business organisation.
2 A drawback of having a long chain of command is that it is difficult to communicate effectively. This is because there are more layers for a message to be passed through. This can mean that subordinates get the wrong or distorted information and could make incorrect decisions.

78. The importance of effective communication

Good communication is important for a business because it ensures that people make the correct decisions and follow the same strategies and principles. Without good communication, employees will make decisions that are not aligned and this can result in different parts of the business not working together, for example, by purchasing the wrong supplies that customers do not want. Another reason for effective communication is that employees want to know what is happening and the direction the business is taking. Without this information, employees will feel insecure and this can lead to demotivation. Good communication will ensure employees feel as though they have a say and are being listened to; this too will help boost motivation.

79. Different ways of working

Remote working describes the ability to work away from the office, such as when out visiting customers or when working from home. Employees can still communicate with the business and access the information they need to do their jobs.

80. Different job roles and responsibilities

A business may employ team leaders to ensure employees are doing their job well. A team leader will supervise work and help employees make corrections and limit the number of mistakes being made. This will help the business lower its costs and increase productivity.

81. Effective recruitment

A person specification is a list of personal qualities, qualifications, experience and skills that are linked to a job role. These factors may be identified as 'essential' or 'desirable'.

82. Developing employees

C

83. The importance of training

A business might choose not to train its employees if it believes they already have the skills necessary to do the job effectively. This might be the case if it has an experienced workforce or has invested heavily in training in the past. Another reason is that the business might be facing financial difficulty. If this is the case, training is often the first thing that a business may cut back on in order to make a saving so that it can spend this money on improving the product or advertising the business.

84. Motivating employees 1

A piece rate system is good because it encourages employees to produce as many units as possible. This is because their pay will be linked to output. As a result, this can help the business increase productivity so that it has more units to sell at a lower average cost.

85. Motivating employees 2

An advantage of job rotation is that workers develop new skills. This means that employees can cover for each other when someone is absent or leaves the organisation. As a result, productivity levels may not fall.

86. Exam skills: Case study

(a) Investors, benefits, competitive market, revenues, operations, competition.
(b) Deliveroo has decided to set wage rates higher the national minimum wage. Employees can earn up to £16 per hour.
(c) Benefits might include:
- workers are classed as self-employed (no obligation to pay employee benefits)
- large potential market
- minimal cost of expanding the business.
Drawbacks might include:
- difficult to differentiate service
- difficult to control level of customer service provided by delivery riders
- new competition from large multinational businesses such as Uber.

87. Exam skills: Short-answer questions

Using self-employed cyclists and drivers means that Deliveroo does not need to pay for staff benefits such as pensions and fringe benefits. This reduces the business's costs, which allows it to compete with delivery companies such as UPS.

88. Exam skills: 'Calculate' questions
31.38%

89. Exam skills: 'Analyse' questions
The use of self-employed workers will keep Deliveroo's staff costs low because the business does not have to provide self-employed workers with the same benefits as permanent employees. It also ensures that the business can act quickly to scale up or down in response to market demand. This could have an impact on the business's success because it could otherwise take too long to hire extra permanent employees and it is easier to stop employing self-employed workers than it would be to downsize if the business found that it had too many permanent employees. However, self-employed workers are less likely to care about the future of the business and may not work as hard or be as motivated as permanent employees, and this could have an impact on the success of the business.

90. Exam skills: 'Justify' questions
Raising share capital by listing on the stock exchange and selling shares to shareholders could finance Deliveroo's expansion plans. The business has been very successful and existing market trends suggest that the market will continue to grow. This means that it is likely to attract lots of potential shareholders and have the ability to raise a lot of money. However, having shareholders will have an impact on the business's management, as they will need to consider the needs and wants of shareholders when making business decisions. Raising funds through crowd funding is unlikely to raise enough money for Deliveroo to finance expansion into a new market. This is because crowd funding is based on the idea that lots of ordinary people invest quite small amounts. Deliveroo is unlikely to attract this sort of investor because it is a large business that has already successfully raised a lot of venture capital. In addition, public concern and media attention about its practice of using self-employed workers rather than permanent staff may make people less likely to invest through crowd funding.

Overall, I think that Option 1 (raising additional share capital from investors) is the most appropriate method that Deliveroo could use to finance its expansion plans, as it is more likely to raise enough finance than via Option 2 (crowd funding). However, selling shares to shareholders can have an impact on management decision-making, which the business's senior leaders may wish to avoid.

91. Exam skills: 'Evaluate' questions
However, there are risks associated with not providing workers with the same benefits and working conditions as those of permanent employees. It may mean that workers are less motivated to provide excellent customer service, because they do not feel invested in the business and do not feel that the business values them. It may also mean that workers are willing to stop working for Deliveroo in order to work for other businesses or new start-ups in the same market, which would have a significant impact on Deliveroo's ability to meet customer demand and continue to fend off the threats posed by potential new entrants such as Uber.

Published by Pearson Education Limited, 80 Strand, London, WC2R 0RL.

www.pearsonschoolsandfecolleges.co.uk

Copies of official specifications for all Pearson qualifications may be found on the website:
qualifications.pearson.com

Text and illustrations © Pearson Education Ltd 2017
Typeset and illustrated by Kamae Design, Oxford
Produced by Out of House Publishing
Cover illustration by Miriam Sturdee

The right of Andrew Redfern to be identified as author of this work has been asserted by him in accordance
with the Copyright, Designs and Patents Act 1988.

First published 2017

20 19 18 17

10 9 8 7 6 5 4 3 2

British Library Cataloguing in Publication Data
A catalogue record for this book is available from the British Library

ISBN 978 1 292 19071 6

Printed in Slovakia by Neografia

Acknowledgements
Text and image on page 43 supplied with kind permission of The Wood Fired Pizza Company
www.woodfiredpizzacompany.co.uk; Image on page 76 reproduced with permission from *CSP Magazine*
http://www.cspdailynews.com/print/csp-magazine/article/menu-heat-seekers-2015?page=0%2C4;
Graph on page 86 reproduced with permission from The NPD Group/CREST®, year ending June 2015.

The author and publisher would like to thank the following individuals and organisations for permission to
reproduce photographs:

(Key: b-bottom; c-centre; l-left; r-right; t-top)

123RF: Antonio Guillem 01, SergiiGalkin 40, Evgenii Andreev 71, Auremar 83, Prig Morisse 84; **Alamy
Stock Photo**: Picturelibrary 16l, Ton Koene 16r, MediaWorldImages 23, Paul Martin 30, Purple Marbles 39,
Homeland photos 56, Martin Bond 58, Studiomode 64, David J. Green 67l, Wu Kailiang 67r, View Pictures
Ltd 85, Clare Jackson 86; **Getty Images:** Scott Olson 69r; **Shutterstock:** Ruth Black 14, OtnaYdur 67c,
Kondor83 69l, Hurst Photo 78l, Bikeriderlondon 78r, Racorn 81

All other images © Pearson Education

Notes from the publisher
1. While the publishers have made every attempt to ensure that advice on the qualification and its assessment
is accurate, the official specification and associated assessment guidance materials are the only authoritative
source of information and should always be referred to for definitive guidance.

Pearson examiners have not contributed to any sections in this resource relevant to examination papers for
which they have responsibility.

2. Pearson has robust editorial processes, including answer and fact checks, to ensure the accuracy of the
content in this publication, and every effort is made to ensure this publication is free of errors. We are,
however, only human, and occasionally errors do occur. Pearson is not liable for any misunderstandings
that arise as a result of errors in this publication, but it is our priority to ensure that the content is accurate.
If you spot an error, please do contact us at resourcescorrections@pearson.com so we can make sure it is
corrected.